How to Pass
THE CIVIL SERVICE
QUALIFYING
TESTS

35/.3 (Full)

How to Pass
THE CIVIL SERVICE
QUALIFYING
TESTS

Mike Bryon

KOGAN
PAGE

This book is dedicated to Stan Bryon who, after a brave fight against cancer, died 2nd April 1994.

First published in 1995

Kogan Page Limited
120 Pentonville Road
London N1 9JN

© Mike Bryon 1995

British Library Cataloguing in Publication Data

A CIP record for this book is available from the British Library.

ISBN 0-7494-1522-3

Printed in England by Clays Ltd, St Ives plc
Typeset by Saxon Graphics Ltd, Derby

Contents

Acknowledgements

Many of the exercises contained in this book have been used to assist groups of students prepare for the Civil Service qualifying tests. I am grateful for their helpful comments and suggestions. I must also thank my colleagues at MBA Training Research Development Ltd and employees of our clients who made the development of this material possible and who have provided much advice and expertise. I owe particular thanks to Bruce Bush and Ian Whittaker for helping in the development of practice questions and Tol Bedford and Neil Scott of Recruitment and Assessment Services (RAS) for useful conversations.

The reason this volume will succeed in its aim to provide advice and assistance to candidates facing RAS exams is that it has been produced with the kind assistance of RAS. Without that it would be far less effective. The copyright to the contents of RAS exams and other publications remain under Crown copyright and I do not assert myself as the author of material which is directly indebted to those publications. The views expressed are entirely my own.

Preface

This text aims to provide advice and practice relevant to the Recruitment and Assessment Service's tests used to recruit administrators to many departments and agencies in the UK Civil Service. The practice exercises are intended to help build up speed, accuracy and confidence in these widely used qualifying exams. The examples may not always reflect the difficulty of the questions in the real tests.

At the time of going to print the material was relevant to the demands of the qualifying exams used to recruit to the posts of Administrative Assistant, Administrative Officer and Executive Officer or their equivalent under new grading structures. Material is also included which is relevant to most parts of the more challenging and difficult Fast Stream exams.

For the recruitment of administrators the majority of Civil Service departments and agencies use the RAS tests. However, other tests are used for the selection of specialist personnel, such as lawyers, engineers and scientists, and these are not dealt with in this book.

In recent years the Civil Service has been subjected to considerable change. You may well have heard of some of these in the news and press, when reference is made, for example, to the Next Steps Initiative and the Citizens' Charter. Every aspect of the Service has been affected, including recruitment practice and the use of qualifying tests.

These days, individual departments have far greater autonomy and some have chosen not to use the RAS tests but instead to develop alternatives of their own. The largest to have done this is the Employment Service and it is important you realise that the material in this book may not be relevant to the tests used by this department. It remains to be seen how this will change, now that the Employment Service is to be merged with the Department for Education.

It is common for job-seekers to take measures to improve their CV or interview technique but relatively few seek to improve their performance in employers' tests. Too few candidates realise that they can improve their scores. It is all too commonly assumed that performance is determined purely by the extent to which you inherently possess or lack a particular aptitude or ability. In fact, you have considerable influence over the test result and you are putting yourself at a disadvantage if you fail to realise this.

Occupational psychologists accept that a lack of familiarity with tests, low self-esteem, nervousness or a lack of confidence will result in a lower score. It is equally true to say that hard work, determination and, most of all, systematic preparation can lead to an improvement in performance.

It is in both your own and an employer's interest that all candidates are given the opportunity to do their best. In this respect, readily available practice questions can make an important contribution, as they allow candidates better to demonstrate their potential. It is obvious and well known that the practice material likely to produce the greatest advantage must be similar to the questions contained in the real test.

This book has been devised expressly for the purpose of helping candidates prepare for the RAS qualifying tests. Clearly, if you face one of these tests then this specialised book promises to be of great help. However, there are important limitations and you must take these into account when deciding on which material you are to practise. In particular, and before you use this book, you must establish that the practice questions are relevant to the test you are going to take. The department or agency to whom you applied should have sent you a description of the test. It is essential that you study this document carefully and establish that this book contains relevant practice material.

I have taken care to provide questions which are relevant to the most common tests currently used but it is possible that, since going to print, the test, or parts of it, will have changed. It is also possible that you have applied to a department which does not use RAS tests and therefore you will face a test which comprises different types of questions. At the end of this volume a list of other sources of practice material is provided (see 'Further Reading' on page 125).

If this book or the suggested further reading does not contain relevant material then contact your local Careers Service, who often hold a library of practice questions. In addition, university and college careers offices will be provided with a computer-based self-assessment package by the start of the academic year 1995–96. These have been developed by RAS for Fast Stream candidates and include sample tests which can be completed to time. Alternatively, write to me, care of Kogan Page, 120 Pentonville Road, London N1 9JN enclosing a copy of the test and a telephone number where you can be contacted. I cannot guarantee that I can help but if I know of any sources I shall be glad to inform you.

When used to select and reject applicants, tests leave the candidate with no alternative but to try and earn the best possible score. Two things will help you to do this. First, it is important that you realise that practice prior to the test will help you to become familiar with the test's demands, build up speed and avoid common mistakes. Second, you must realise that doing well in a test is not simply down to intelligence but also requires you to be sufficiently motivated to want to pass and to try hard. In some cases, practice and a determination to do well will mean the difference between pass and fail.

Chapter 1

Administrative Staff in the Civil Service

Civil servants are officials who work for a Minister of the government of the day. They work in departments and agencies of central government, developing and implementing policies. Employees of the police, local government, the armed forces or nationalised industries are not civil servants.

Civil servants are politically impartial and the Service is non-political. Governments change but the Service remains unaffected and will serve whichever government is elected.

In recent years the Service has undergone considerable change, and previously centrally defined structures will no longer necessarily apply throughout the Service. Increasingly, civil servants are occupied with the development and implementation of the policies of the European Union as well as those of Parliament.

In 1988 the Next Steps initiative was launched and has been responsible for the decentralisation of responsibility and the creation of executive agencies. An agency, such as the Benefits Agency, is a body within a government department and concerned with the day-to-day delivery of a service but not its strategic control.

The Citizens' Charter initiative has also brought considerable change. The aim is to raise the quality of public service. Citizens' Charters affect both civil servants and employees of local government and organisations such as the Health Service.

A major effort has been made to locate parts of departments and most of the executive agencies outside the capital.

This has meant that fewer civil servants are located in London and the south-east region in fact the percentage of all civil servants working is London now stands at 20 per cent.

Up to now, the terms and conditions of employment and rights and responsibilities of civil servants are very clearly structured and defined. The Civil Service Staff Handbook that explains most of these regulations is a substantial, rigorous and clearly written document which is available to all employees. Although in recent years the prospects for promotion have reduced considerably, all staff benefit from annual appraisals which include an assessment of whether or not the individual is fit for promotion.

It is a legal requirement that recruitment to the Service is by fair and open competition and that selection and promotion is on the basis of merit alone. The Service is an acknow ledged leader in the provision of child care support, career-break schemes and job-sharing arrangements. I have first-hand experience of working with civil servants who take equality of opportunity very seriously and work hard to ensure a fair and equitable system of recruitment and management.

Despite these best efforts, the Service has experienced difficulties with the implementation of equal opportunities. Few departments, for example, achieved the requirement of the 1944 Disabled Persons Act under which 3 per cent of its staff should be registered disabled (employers are likely to be relieved of this requirement in a proposed amendment to the Act currently being debated by government).

Evidence relating to 1992 suggested that black and other ethnic minority people within the Service were more likely to be employed in the clerical grades. The proportion of women civil servants in posts classified grade 7 or above was found to be considerably lower than the total should be if the sexes were proportionally represented. There have been considerable and genuine efforts, coordinated by the Cabinet Office, to address these issues of representation.

No system is perfect and there is still important work to be done before equality of opportunity is fully realised. The Service, however, is ahead of the majority of Britain's industries and represents a better employer than most.

Administrators in the Service are in an important respect considered to be generalists. After a qualifying period, and once you reach the higher grades, you may gain experience of all aspects of administration and be moved between specialist functions periodically. The experience gained in each function is judged to be transferable and you will be expected to be able to learn quickly and be flexible. Training is primarily on the job. The key functions include work in, for example, a registry, a secretariat, a finance section, a personnel or training department or a computing unit.

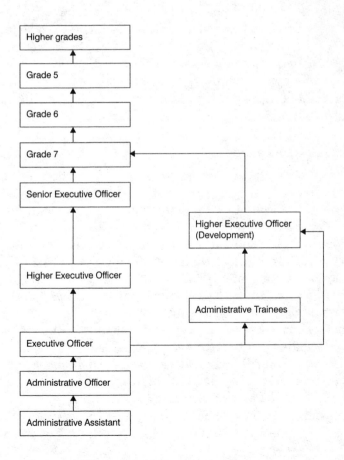

There used to be a well-defined career path which can be pictorially represented as shown in the diagram.

As an administrative entrant into the Service you could start your career in one of the following grades (or their equivalents):

Administrative Assistant

Administrative Assistants keep and update records both on paper and on computers, maintain filing systems, open the post, write standard letters, answer telephone or face-to-face enquiries, take messages, operate office equipment such as a photocopier and maintain supplies.

The criteria used in recruitment to the post requires two GCSE passes at grade C or equivalent qualifications, one of which must be English Language. If you lack these qualifications or evidence of them then you may be invited to take the clerical test (see Chapter 3).

Equivalent qualifications from Britain, the European Union and Commonwealth countries are accepted. Note that the department or agency will want to see the original certificate for all qualifications.

Administrative Officer

Administrative Officers perform many of the functions of the Administrative Assistant, such as the answering of written, telephone or face-to-face enquiries and the maintenance of both paper and computer records. However, they are required to show initiative and make decisions. They may monitor statistics and personnel and financial records and be responsible for the interpretation of those records and the instigation of particular action. They may also be responsible for the handling of quite large sums of money.

The criteria used for the selection of an Administrative Officer requires you to have five GCSEs at grade C or above, one of which must be English Language. Alternatively, you may be promoted from the grade of Administrative Assistant or be expected to pass the clerical test (see Chapter 3).

Equivalent British qualifications and those from the European Union and Commonwealth countries are accepted.

Executive Officer (or equivalent)

This is the main graduate entry grade to the Civil Service. In fact, half the candidates recruited at this level are graduates. Executive Officers manage staff and are often expected to lead a small team. They must be able to specialise and adjust to the challenge of a new role quickly and with confidence. Much of their work is carried out with very little supervision. Their work may involve travel anywhere in the United Kingdom or abroad. They write reports and make important decisions which may involve large sums of public money or carry considerable responsibility.

The criteria used for the selection of staff to this grade usually require you to hold a minimum of five GCSEs including two at A level, all at grade C or higher, and one must be English Language. Equivalent qualifications from the UK, European Union and Commonwealth countries are accepted. A degree is accepted as an equivalent. An age requirement of between 17½ and 55 years is sometimes applied. You may also be expected to pass the Executive Officer qualification test (see Chapter 4). Internal candidates can be promoted from the grade of Administrative Officer.

Administration Trainee and Higher Executive Officer (Development)

These positions are referred to as the Fast Stream, and competition for them is very tough. In 1993/94 there were approximately 140 places and 11,000 applicants. Only 700 applicants make it past both the sift at the application stage and the one day of qualifying tests. Many applicants mistakenly see this grade as the main point of graduate entry but, as we have seen, far more graduates start a career in the grade of Executive Officer.

For the first few years entrants receive formal and on-the-job training. After that you are considered for what is called 'accelerated promotion'. Typically, the work involves research and analysis of policy, management of major projects or the support of Ministers. You can expect to manage your own staff.

There is a specialist European Fast Stream which aims to prepare, annually, around 30 people (under the age of 32) for the recruitment competitions to the European Commission.

To qualify for entry into the Fast Stream competition, candidates are required to have a minimum of a second-class honours degree or equivalent. (Practice for the Fast Stream test is provided in Chapter 6.)

Information for applicants

The Service goes to considerable lengths to provide detailed information to applicants about vacancies and the recruitment process to be adopted. To illustrate further the type of work involved, the details of the terms and conditions of employment and the selection process, I have reproduced two examples of the type of information sent out to applicants to recent specific vacancies. Please note that these are only two of many hundreds of examples and that conditions of employment may vary from department to department and from post to post. In particular, note that not all departments or agencies operate such strict nationality, immigration or security requirements.

The post of Administrative Assistant with the Home Office and Prison Service

Information for Applicants

Applications are invited to fill a number of Administrative Assistants vacancies within the Home Office based in central London and the Prison Service based in central London and Croydon.

These posts are permanent and pensionable.

Your completed application form and biodata response sheet should be completed and returned by 19 December 1994.

The Home Office

The Home Office is an historic Department of State concerned with domestic policy over a wide range of issues which affect the lives and liberties of individual citizens and the good order of society.

The Home Office is widely regarded as the 'Law and Order Department' and is primarily concerned with: the administration of justice; criminal law; the treatment of offenders, including probation; the prison service; the police; crime prevention; fire and emergency planning; passports; immigration and nationality; certain public safety matters and race relations.

Among the various other matters with which the Home Office deals are: gambling; the liquor licensing law; the control of fire arms and dangerous drugs; preparing patents of nobility for peers and formal proceedings for the bestowal of honours; extradition of criminals; church matters; scrutinising local authority by-laws; granting licences for scientific experiments on animals; burial, exhumation and cremation; and British Summer Time.

The Prison Service

The Prison Service is responsible for the management of all prisons, remand centres and young offender institutions in England and Wales. The Prisons Board comprises the Director General, two Operational Directors, the Director of Services, the Director of Personnel, the Director of Finance and the Director of Health Care and four non-executive directors. The two operational directorates combine responsibility for the operational management of establishments with responsibility for various aspects of Prison Service policy. Establishments are grouped in areas. Each area manager is responsible for eight or nine establishments and he or she reports direct to an operational director on the performance of the Service's principal functions – to hold prisoners committed to custody by the courts and to provide inmates with work, education, physical exercise, spiritual and emotional support and the opportunity to develop social skills before they return to society.

The job

Administrative Assistants will be required to undertake a range of general administrative duties including: keeping of records – often involving using the VDU; sorting and filing papers; data entry; figure work – perhaps using a calculator; dealing with written or telephone enquiries form the public.

Age

There are no formal age limits. But in deciding your suitability for appointment the Home Office or the Prison Service would need to ensure that the period of service you will be able to give, having regard to the normal retiring age of 60, would be sufficient to recoup training and induction costs. Candidates aged 55 or over are therefore considerably less likely to be appointed unless they possess exceptional experience.

Disabled persons

The Disabled Persons (Employment) Act 1944 defines a disabled person in the following terms: A person who on account of injury, disease or congenital deformity is substantially handicapped in obtaining or keeping employment or in undertaking work on his/her own account, of a kind which, apart from that injury, disease or congenital deformity, would be suited to his/her age, experience and qualification.

Nationality and immigration control

You should normally be a British or Commonwealth Citizen (as defined in the British Nationality Act 1981), a British protected person, or a national of a state within the European Economic Area. If you are unsure of your status, please explain your circumstances in a letter accompanying your application.

Entry to the United Kingdom is controlled under the Immigration Act 1971. Everyone who does not have the right of abode is subject to immigration control. You should check whether there are any restrictions on your stay or your freedom to take or change employment before you apply for a post.

If you would like further information on this topic, please write to RAS Mailing Services, Alencon Link, Basingstoke, Hants RG21 1JB or telephone (01256) 468551.

Security

The posts covered by this scheme of recruitment require security clearance.

If you are selected for interview you will be asked to complete a security questionnaire which will explain the government's vetting policy.

Candidates are normally required to have a minimum period of residence in the United Kingdom before they can be considered for security clearance. The period of residence required is three years, including candidates who were born in the United Kingdom.

Salary

Starting salary will depend on the extent and quality of relevant experience you are able to offer and will be in the range £4,995 (at age 16) to £7,421. If you are aged 16 on entry you will receive an annual increment until you reach the age of 18. Progression up the pay scale will depend on performance, up to a current maximum of £10,164 in the Home Office and £10,408 in the Prison Service.

In addition, these posts currently attract an annual allowance of £1,776 for posts in Central London and £1,015 for posts in Croydon. You are advised, however, that this allowance is not an entitlement and the amount paid may be withdrawn or amended at any time.

Personal qualities

You need to be a good communicator and possess good organisational and interpersonal skills. You should be adaptable and able to work on your own initiative.

The ability to work as part of a team is essential as is coping well with changing situations and when the pressure is on. An aptitude for IT would be an advantage as, once in post, it is expected that you will be able to use IT equipment after instruction.

Hours and leave

You will normally work a 5 day week of 36 hours excluding lunch intervals.

The annual leave allowance is 4 weeks and 2 days rising to 5 weeks after 1 year's service and 6 weeks after 20 years total service.

Pensions

Unless you choose otherwise, pension benefits are provided under the Principal Civil Service Pension Scheme (PCSPS), which is contracted out of the state scheme. It is non-contributory, apart from 1.5% of salary for widow's/widower's benefits which are refundable if you are unmarried when your service ends.

Selection

The candidates who appear from the information available to be most suited will be invited to sit a test designed to test their aptitude for administration work.

Illustrated examples will be sent with the invitation to the test which will be held in London during the week commencing 9 January 1995.

Those who are qualified will be invited to an interview which will be held in London during February 1995 and last about 30 minutes.

The Selection Board will normally consist of 2/3 interviewers who will question you mainly on subjects connected with your work experience and interests, as well as on a few topics of general interest and current affairs.

Pre-appointment enquiries

If you are recommended for appointment, enquiries will be carried out into your health and other matters, to ensure that you are qualified for appointment. To enable these enquiries to be completed, we may need to see your original birth certificate and/or passport. When the enquiries are completed satisfactorily, it will be for the Home Office or the Prison Service to make you a formal offer of appointment.

Application

Your completed Application Form and biodata response sheet should reach Recruitment and Assessment Services, Room 201, Alencon Link, Basingstoke, Hants RG21 1JB by 19 December 1994. Earlier receipt would be helpful. Please note that we are unable to accept application forms received after the closing date.

Applications received without the original biodata response sheet will not be accepted.

If you wish to have your application form acknowledged would you please, before returning it, write your name and full postal address on the acknowledgement card provided, affix an appropriate postage stamp, and return the card with the completed forms. The card will be posted back to you.

Equal opportunities

Applications are invited from candidates regardless of ethnic origin, religious belief, gender, sexual orientation, disability or other irrelevant factor. People with disabilities and those from ethnic minorities are currently under-represented and their applications are particularly welcome.

The post of Executive Officer with the Cabinet Office

Multi-departmental Executive Officer recruitment scheme

Applications are invited to fill a number of Executive Officer vacancies within the Export Credits Guarantee Department based in London. Other vacancies may arise in due course.

These posts are permanent and pensionable.

Your completed application form and biodata response sheet should be completed and returned by 13 July 1995.

Background

ECGD – The Export Credits Guarantee Department – is a Government Department, created in 1919 to promote UK exports by insuring them against the risks of non-payment by overseas buyers. Since then they have insured over £260bn of exports and have an annual turnover of around £3.5bn. ECGD are based in London's Docklands with supporting staff in Cardiff, and employ around 500 people

ECGD is regulated by an Act of Parliament – the Export and Investment Guarantees Act 1991 – and is answerable to the Secretary of State for Trade and Industry.

Aims

ECGD offers three basic services to the exporting community:

- **guarantees** of payment to banks providing export finance;
- **support** for export finance at favourable fixed interest rates;
- **insurance** for non-payment on export contracts.

ECGD provide support for business in the project, capital goods, construction and services sectors of the economy. Much of this business involves long delivery periods and/or credit requirements. Two to ten years credit is typical.

Their services take away many of the payment risks and enable exporters to make sales more boldly by taking on new buyers and breaking into new markets. They also help people win business by enabling them to offer competitive credit terms.

ECGD gives banks who provide export finance an unconditional guarantee of repayment. It also insures exporters against the main commercial and political risks which arise during the manufacturing and credit periods. **Commercial** risks are those connected with the buyer, such as insolvency or default; **Political** risks are broadly those outside an individual's control, such as hard currency shortages, war or civil unrest. Although ECGD is a Government Department, they are expected to run their credit insurance operations as a business, generating sufficient reserves to give the level of assurance of breaking even that Ministers require. Applying normal insurance principles, ECGD assess the risk on each contract individually. This means examining each project, buyer or borrower and country risk. In 1991, the Portfolio Management System was introduced to assess risk more systematically, match premium to risk and balance the national interest reasons for supporting project exports with the risk to the taxpayer of having to meet any shortfall between premium income and claims payments.

Following the privatisation of their short term insurance business in December 1991, this cover is now provided entirely by the private sector and prospective customers should seek the advice of their broker.

Job Description

The main duties and responsibilities of an Executive Officer within ECGD lie in the categories listed below:

1. *Management*

   The Executive Officer (EO) grade is the first level at which management and supervision are likely to constitute a significant part of the work. Postholders will have responsibility for integrating various tasks and ensuring the work is completed in accordance with instructions and required timetables. EOs will be concerned with making the best use of staff and other resources.

2. *Policy*

   Postholders will be responsible for researching subjects, analysing information and identifying relevant features and submitting recommendations. This includes, for example, providing the first drafts of briefs and responses to Parliamentary Questions.

3. *Casework*

   Where the application of rules and regulations is involved the EO may be the main working level. Duties will involve, for example, the scrutiny of material and/or the application of regulations to specific areas. An EO may lead a small team involved on casework where much of the work can be undertaken at a lower level, or they may themselves be members of casework teams involved with, for example, investigations or the adjudication of more difficult cases.

4. *Specialist*

   In areas such as Information Technology (IT), Inspectorial, Audit and Finance, postholders may work as members of teams or in singleton posts providing the appropriate specialist support, undertaking research and investigation, analysing results and submitting recommendations to clients.

5. *Representation*

   Many jobs undertaken by EOs involve regular face to face contact with people from outside their own departments. Some will have considerable contact (frequently, daily) with members of the public, private industry and local government, for example, in the office and at traders' premises when answering enquiries and offering advice on rules and regulations. EOs may also, on occasions, negotiate on behalf of the Department in a limited area where constraints have been agreed previously.

Person Specification

The characteristics of the work at EO level require postholders to exercise judgement and interpretative ability where the work falls within clearly defined rules and regulations and where past precedent and experience is generally available. Postholders will have to deal with a range of problems/decisions, which will require them to select the appropriate course of action from a number of options. In the light of acquired experience and knowledge they will be expected to exercise a judgement. In some specialist posts, they will also need to use professional knowledge gained from formal study and/or practical training. In certain posts they may undertake work which has a direct bearing on the acquisition of formal qualifications.

Educational Qualifications*

It is not practicable to list all of them. Basically the main acceptable educational qualifications are set out below:

1. A university or CNAA degree or a Higher National Certificate/Diploma; or
2. 5 GCE/GCSEs in acceptable grades including English Language of which 2 must be at 'A' level; or
3. 4 SCE Higher passes including English or 5 SCE passes including English with 3 of the passes at the Higher grade; or
4. Ordinary National Certificate/Diploma (plus 4 acceptable 'O' level passes – or Scottish equivalent or BTEC General Diploma (credit level) or BTEC First Diploma (pass); or
5. Qualifications considered to be of an equivalent standard to those already mentioned.

*Requirements may differ for existing civil servants.

Nationality

These are non public service posts, open to British or Commonwealth Citizens (as defined in the British Nationality Act 1981), British protected persons, or nationals of a state within the European Economic Area. If you are unsure of your status, please explain your circumstances in a letter accompanying your application.

There must be no employment restrictions or time limit on your stay in the United Kingdom.

Health Standard

For these appointments you must be able to give regular and effective service for at least five years. You will therefore be asked to complete a health declaration and, if necessary, to attend a medical examination.

Disabled Persons

The Disabled Persons (Employment) Act 1944 defines a disabled person in the following terms:

A person who, on account of injury, disease or congenital deformity, is substantially handicapped in obtaining or keeping employment or in undertaking work on his/her own account, of a kind which, apart from that injury, disease or congenital deformity, would be suited to his/her age, experience and qualifications.

Trial Period

You will be on probation for a maximum of one year but in exceptional circumstances this may be extended. If you are already an established civil servant you will revert to your previous grade if your probationary service is unsatisfactory.

Career Development and Prospects

The first step in promotion is to the grade of Higher Executive Officer (HEO). Promotion is based on merit, at least two years' experience in the EO grade is usually required before promotion. Similarly, there is a seniority requirement of two years between the grades of HEO and SEO (Senior Executive Officer). Once this basic experience has been gained, however, promotion to higher grades is based entirely on merit.

Salary

Starting salary will be appropriate to the Executive Officer grade and will be in the range £11,673 to £14,901. In addition, there is a Recruitment and Retention Allowance (RRA) of £1,776 per annum. It should be advised that RRA is not an entitlement and the amount may be reduced or withdrawn at any time.

Progression is dependent on individual performance.

The salary is paid monthly by credit transfer and increases are normally granted annually subject to performance.

If you are already an established civil servant starting pay will be determined under the rules for starting pay on promotion if you are in a lower grade, or under the rules for regrading if you are in an equivalent or higher grade.

Hours and Leave

You will normally work a 5 day week of 41 hours including lunch intervals. A flexible working hours system is in operation.

The annual leave allowance is 22 days rising to 25 days after 1 year's total service and 30 days after 20 years total service. In addition to the above you will receive 10½ days public and privilege holidays to be taken at specified times of the year.

Pension

Unless you choose otherwise, your appointment will be pensionable under the Principal Civil Service Pension Scheme (PCSPS), which is contracted out of the state scheme. It is non-contributory, apart from 1½% of salary for widow's /widower's benefits which are refundable if you are unmarried when your service ends.

Selection

The candidates who appear from the information available to have the best qualifications and experience will be invited to sit a test designed to test aptitude for Executive Officer work.

If you have taken the Selection Test within the last 12 months you may be exempt from the tests for this scheme and use your previous score. However, there can be no guarantee that such a score would be sufficient, on this occasion, to enable you to proceed to interview. (Your score will be verified by RAS.)

Illustrative examples will be sent with the invitation to the test which will be held during early August 1995 in London.

Those who qualify will be invited to an interview which will last about 30 minutes. There will be 3 interviewers who will question you mainly on subjects connected with your academic and/or work experience and interests, as well as on a few topics of general interest and current affairs. The interviews will be held in London in late August 1995.

Pre-appointment Enquiries

If you are recommended for appointment, enquiries will be carried out into your nationality, health and other matters, to ensure that you are qualified for appointment. To enable these enquiries to be completed, we will need to see your original birth certificate and/or passport, as well as your educational certificates. When the enquiries are completed satisfactorily, it will be for the Department to make you a formal offer of appointment.

Application

Your completed Application Form should reach Recruitment & Assessment Services, Room 201, Alençon Link, Basingstoke, Hants RG21 7JB by 13 July 1995. Earlier receipt would be helpful. **Please note that we will be unable to accept application forms received after the closing date.**

If you wish to have your application form acknowledged would you please, before returning it, write your name and full postal address on the acknowledgement card provided, affix an appropriate postage stamp, and return the card with the completed forms. The card will then be posted back to you.

If you need to contact us:

Telephone Bernie Barton:	01256 846422
Fax:	01256 846478
Please quote ref:	C/96/0638/004

Applicants who are not successful through this scheme of recruitment will be considered for inclusion in the new recruitment database.

Equal Opportunity

It is government policy to provide equal opportunity for employment, career development and promotion in the Civil Service to all who are eligible, on the basis of ability, qualifications and fitness for the work. All government departments and agencies are wholeheartedly committed to this policy. Applications are welcome from all qualified individuals irrespective of race, sex, marital status or disability.

Chapter 2

Tests and Practice

The challenge of an open and fair recruitment policy

It was mentioned in the previous chapter that the Civil Service has a legal requirement to recruit by fair and open competition and to select applicants on the basis of merit alone. Fairness and openness mean that the Service is required to ensure that vacancies are advertised and all eligible candidates may apply.

These twin aims, although laudable, create difficulties. To ensure openness, vacancies are widely publicised and, consequently, often result in very large numbers of applications. To ensure fairness each application must be given proper and due consideration which takes a considerable amount of time. The cost and time it takes to scrutinise large numbers of applications can become a serious problem and becomes more urgent as the number of applications increases.

Faced with this problem RAS has adopted a recruitment process which comprises a number of key features, some of which have been described in Chapter 1:

- All applicants are sent information about the work so that they can make an informed decision over whether or not to proceed with their application.
- Application forms have been adopted which obtain sufficient information to afford a sift against a set of criteria agreed in advance and considered essential to the post.
- Candidates who pass the application form sift may be requested to pass a set of standardised tests which are administered to large groups of applicants at a time.

- Panel interviews are conducted.

The value of tests

The predictive validity of tests

All employers' tests, including those used by the Civil Service and developed by RAS, owe much of their heritage to attempts early this century to measure intelligence.

We are all familiar with the notion of IQ (Intelligence Quotient) and how a single score is offered as a measurement of an individual's intelligence; a score of 100 is deemed average, while a score of over 160 might indicate a genius.

Pioneers of testing predicted that we would no longer have to wait for the effects of experience to discover how well suited an individual was for a particular career or educational path. Instead, we would be able to attribute to an individual a single score and be able to tell who was best suited for particular careers and higher education, and so sort people into the appropriate slot in society. The US during the early 1920s saw the general public become 'IQ conscious' and group intelligence testing become widespread.

It was soon realised that these early IQ tests failed to measure intelligence or predict success in higher education and a person's suitability for a particular career. Intelligence is a controversial notion which has proved very difficult to define. The concept of intelligence adopted by the early testers was crude and only a few items which are purported to make up this complex term were employed. The early tests were primarily concerned with the measurement of verbal ability and the ability to handle numerical, pictorial and geometric relations.

The overstatement of the validity of these early tests gave rise to considerable scepticism and hostility towards testing. Lasting harm was done to the testing industry and remained an important influence on the development of later tests. There had, of course, been more sober commentators and the views of these individuals came to the fore. In particular, it was stressed that an individual's score should not be taken as an indication of overall intelligence but instead simply as a measurement of that individual's ability in the aptitude tested. Some IQ tests were renamed ability tests and redesigned to measure specific aptitudes. Instead of attributing a single score, a profile of scores in each ability was offered. In other cases an individual's score was simply compared with the normal score of other candidates with a similar background. These tests are in essence the precursors to the tests used today by employers. Considerable and lengthy studies are undertaken in order to quantify the predictive value of such tests.

Are tests valid?

I do not want to get too embroiled in a debate on the predictive validity of psychometric tests. Whether or not you believe them to be valid hardly matters. All that counts is that employers use them and if you apply for a career and the recruitment process includes a test then you have little choice but to take it or abandon your choice of employer.

It may be helpful, however, if we briefly consider a number of practical limitations which affect validity. In particular, I am interested in issues which will help to put in context the significance of your own test performance and illustrate the limitations to what can be inferred from a pass or fail in a psychometric test.

Tests apply scientific methodology to recruitment

Recruitment is a notoriously subjective business. Handwriting analysis, personality questionnaires, application forms, references and interviews all fail to discriminate objectively between candidates. The best we can say is that some of these methods are less subjective than others. The occupational psychologist, however, goes to considerable lengths to achieve objectivity and he or she does this by applying standard scientific methods and statistical techniques to the task of deciding between candidates. The resulting psychometric tests are considered by many to be the best single predictor of likely job performance.

This is not to say that tests are perfect. In fact, the vast majority of tests are imperfect because, for most positions, job performance is ill defined. Things are made worse because the contents of most tests – the questions of which they are comprised – do not exactly measure the behavioural traits under investigation. They also inadvertently measure traits which are irrelevant to the post.

As a test candidate, the most important thing to realise about the subjectivity of tests is that they will produce what are called 'false negative' and 'false positive' results. An imperfect test will not exactly predict job performance. This will mean that the true potential of some candidates will be under-estimated while the potential of others will be over-estimated. If someone capable of doing the job is falsely attributed a low score and their application is then rejected they are called a 'false negative'. If a candidate achieves a score greater than their true potential and, as a result, they are passed through to the next stage in the recruitment process then they are called 'false positives'.

In practice, large numbers of applicants can make a test almost worthless

We have seen that a successful policy of openness is likely to result in large number of applicants and that this makes the operation of an equitable selection process difficult. This is true in testing as well as in other aspects of a recruitment process. It is true because, when faced with many thousands of candidates, an employer finds it necessary to introduce cut-off points to reduce the number who pass through to the next stage. This is done simply by rejecting all applicants who fall below a particular score or by fixing a limit to the number of applicants allowed through. Cut-off points create further problems with the prediction of job performance because they considerably increase the number of false negatives.

In extreme cases a less-than-perfect test with a very high cut-off point can become almost worthless at predicting job performance. This will occur when many thousands take a test but very few are allowed through to the next stage. In these circumstances, a great number of candidates who have the potential to do the job will fail to achieve the cut-off score, and so will be rejected as false negatives. To make matters worse some successful candidates are likely to be false positives.

The validity of a test when used for selection purposes

An important distinction in the function of psychometric tests is the difference between a test when used for diagnostic purposes and a test when used for selection.

When a test is used for diagnostic purposes you and the test author share the same psychometric goal, namely to measure the extent to which you possess or lack particular abilities. In the diagnostic situation you have an interest in helping to ensure that the test produces the most objective assessment of your strengths and weaknesses. To cheat would only mislead yourself.

Contrast this situation with one when a test is used for selection purposes. The use of a psychometric test in this situation pitches the candidate against the test author. The candidate must get the best possible score and cover up any area of weaknesses if he or she is to pass to the next stage of the recruitment process. Under these circumstances, the test author must produce a test which offers an objective assessment of the candidate's abilities, despite the fact that the candidates are trying to distort the outcome.

When a test is used for selection purposes, test security is of far greater importance. The impact of the effects of coaching on a candidate's score is also of far greater concern to the psychologist.

The effect of you on validity

It is clear from what has just been said on the use of a test for selection as distinct from diagnostic purposes that the candidates and their approach can have an impact on test validity. The effect you have on test value is further evident because if you have not taken many tests before you are likely to do considerably less well than a candidate who is familiar with and practised in them. If English is not your first language, or if you suffer a disability, then a test is even more likely to fail as an indicator of your true potential.

As a candidate you can afford to be sceptical about the predictive value of employers' tests. Notification that you were unsuccessful may mean nothing more than that you were simply a false negative or did not undertake sufficient practice. You should certainly not conclude that failure to pass a qualifying exam means you are not suitable for a particular career. In fact, there is only one certain thing that we can say a test definitely measures and that is the extent to which you successfully answer or fail to answer the questions which it comprises.

It would be a mistake to conclude that failure in an employer's test means that you should rethink your career plans. In some circumstances, however, it would be equally wrong to doggedly follow the maxim that 'if you fail you should try and try again'. If you have repeatedly taken the same test, perhaps year after year, only to fail every time, it is unlikely that your fortune will change and that you will pass one day. In some instances so many people apply for particular work and there are so few vacancies, that even the very able are rejected. In the face of consistent failure you should try to establish if any alternative routes into the employment of your choice exist. It may well be that holders of particular qualifications do not have to sit the test; alternatively, it may be possible to achieve your goal through promotion.

The value of practice

All candidates can improve their scores with practice and in some cases a candidate will improve sufficiently to pass something they would have otherwise failed.

Practice is mostly likely to help if you would otherwise fail by only a few marks. Such people are referred to as 'near-miss candidates'. The biggest gains are achieved by someone who has had little or no previous experience of tests.

In order to maximise the benefit of practice you should undertake two forms of preparation.

1.   You should practise in a relaxed situation, without time constraints, on questions which are similar to those described in the employer's test booklet. The aim is to realise the test demands and build up confidence in your own abilities.

2.   Then practise on realistic questions against a strict time limit and in circumstances as realistic to the test as you can manage. The aim is to get used to answering the questions under the pressure of time and to build up speed and accuracy.

Try to undertake a minimum of 12 hours' practice, or more if you can obtain sufficient practice material. Remember, restrict your practice to questions similar to the real thing.

verning the credit process

>ices are sent out with the goods and state that the
pany operates a strict 20-day credit facility from the
of invoice.

first reminder is sent out 14 days after the goods. If
nent is still not received the second reminder is sent
a further 10 days.

>unt reviews are held 17 days after the issuing of the
nd reminder.

ses when the sum owed exceeds £100 and payment
>t received within 20 days from the date of the
unt review then court action is instigated.

e court case is lost the amount is written off as a bad

out exception credit facilities are withdrawn when
action is initiated or when any sum becomes more
60 days overdue.

nent was received 22 working days after the date
nvoice. What stage of the credit process would
last been implemented?

B	C	D	E	F	G	H	I	J

t action has had to be initiated against a creditor.
t would have been the action taken immediately
to this?

B	C	D	E	F	G	H	I	J

ditor has owed £98 for almost two months. What
 should be taken?

B	C	D	E	F	G	H	I	J

verage time taken for payment to be received is
rking days from the invoice date. What stage of

Chapter 3

Practice for the Clerical Tests

The RAS clerical qualifying test

In 1992 RAS introduced a new paper and pencil clerical test
for recruitment to the posts of Administrative Assistant,
Administrative Officer and equivalent positions. The new
test has been designed to achieve four principal aims,
which RAS describe as follows:

> To be user friendly to applicants from all sections of society. To
> accurately predict applicants' probability of success in the job.
> To assess applicants on the core competencies required by
> administrative staff. To 'look the part'. That is, to use job-
> related language and contexts, without needing any work
> experience to be able to answer the questions.[1]

The new test evolved and was validated through a lengthy
process of development. This involved, for example, volun-
teer civil servants taking the test, in order to establish the
likely score of a candidate capable of doing the job, and
large scale trials on candidates with a variety of back-
grounds so that it could be predicted what the likely score
would be of a candidate with a particular background.
Users of the test are advised not to set too high a pass mark
as this will reduce the predictive value of the test and risk
making it unacceptably subjective.

---

[1] The source of this quote and other information contained in
this account of the clerical test is from *A guide to the new AA/AO
selection test*, published by RAS, 1993. I am grateful to RAS for
allowing me access to this booklet which is intended for the
employees of departments and agencies which use RAS tests.

If you are successful in the initial stage of your application you will receive a letter inviting you to sit the test. This will be accompanied by a booklet containing a useful description of the battery of tests and some example questions. It is important that you study this document. It is worth noting that the booklet states 'no marks are deducted for incorrect answers' and that all the sub-tests are multiple-choice.

Multiple-choice tests present the candidate with a fixed number of suggested answers, one, or sometimes more, of which is or are correct. No points are deducted for incorrect answers in the RAS clerical test. A candidate may therefore improve on his or her score by guessing at the answer to questions if the answer is unknown. So make sure you answer all questions even if this means you spend the last minute guessing answers to the remaining questions.

The number of suggested answers for each question varies between sub-tests. If we take the example of the Numerical Tasks sub-test there are six suggested answers. Assuming that there is only one correct answer, simple guessing would mean that, on average, you would guess right one time in six. You may be able to improve on this if you made educated guesses. This involves looking at the suggested answers and seeing if you can rule any out as incorrect. If you can, you will improve your chances of guessing the correct answer.

To indicate your chosen answer you must make a bold horizontal pencil mark across the appropriate space in the answer box. If you decide to change your chosen answer take care to erase your first answer completely.

> On the day of the test do not forget to take with you any corrective glasses or contact lenses.

Practice exercises

The remainder of this chapter provides practice questions for each of the sub-tests which make up the RAS clerical battery in its current format. Note that in the real test you

will be given separate question book for each of the sub-tests.

The test comprises four sub-tests i one and a half hours. (Answers are chapter.)

Sub-test 1. Following procedure

The RAS test in following procedur to follow explicit rules and interpret

In the real test you are allowed questions and are presented with answers from which you must in Below you will find a practice exer tions. Please note that some of the more than one suggested answer to

A credit management process
The flow diagram below illustrat process.

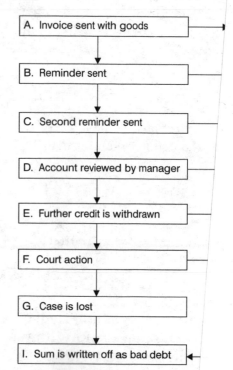

Rules g
1. Inv
   cor
   da
2. The
   pay
   afte
3. Acc
   sec
4. In c
   is r
   acc
5. If th
   deb
6. Witl
   cou
   thar

Question
1. Pay
   of
   hav

   A

2. Cou
   Wh:
   prio

   A

3. A cr
   actic

   A

4. The
   39 w

the process would next be initiated if payment was not received by then?

A   B   C   D   E   F   G   H   I   J

5. Identify which stages could precede a debt being written off as bad.

A   B   C   D   E   F   G   H   I   J

6. A payment has still not been received after 30 days. What action could be taken?

A   B   C   D   E   F   G   H   I   J

7. What are the possible outcomes from court action?

A   B   C   D   E   F   G   H   I   J

8. 20 days have passed since a case review. The sum outstanding is £120. What action should be taken?

A   B   C   D   E   F   G   H   I   J

9. What actions can an account manager recommend?

A   B   C   D   E   F   G   H   I   J

10. Since the date of the invoice 41 days have passed. What action is due to be taken?

A   B   C   D   E   F   G   H   I   J

Sub-test 2. Numerical tasks

The RAS test of numerical tasks comprises 24 numerical questions for which you are allowed 20 minutes. So you need to complete each question in 50 seconds. Six possible answers are offered to each question and labelled alphabetically A, B, C, D, E, F. Only one suggested answer is correct. Your task is to work out which of the six is the correct answer and enter the corresponding letter in the answer box.

To do well in the numerical sub-test you need to be well practised in addition, subtraction, multiplication, division and the working out of percentages. You also need to be confident in the application of decimals, time, money, metric measurements and simple fractions. Try the 12 practice questions below. If you are unable to do them, or you get some wrong, you should work hard on your arithmetic before you take the clerical exam. You will find many more of this type of practice question in Maths GCSE revision books.

Do not use a calculator or other mechanical aid. In the real exam you are provided with rough paper for working out.

1. $720 + 200 + 0.1$ =   ?   _____

2. $13.2 - 9.6$ =   ?   _____

3. 248×7 =   ?   _____

4. 2.56×0.4 =   ?   _____

5. 1050 divided by 5   =   ?   _____

6. $\frac{1}{2} + 1\frac{1}{4}$ =   ?   _____

7. 65% of 256   =   ?   _____

8. $200 \times ?\%$ =   100   _____

9. If 66 is 11% what is 100%?   _____

10. How many minutes are there in two and a quarter hours? _____

11. How many centimetres are there in one and a third metres? _____

12. How many grams are there in three two-kilo bags of sugar? _____

Now try the following 23 questions which are in the same format as the questions in the real sub-test. Practise in order to build up your speed, confidence and accuracy or to revise forgotten rules of arithmetic. Do look at the suggested answers to see if you can save time by estimating the answers. Where it helps, round sums up or down to more convenient amounts. If you cannot work out a question, practise educated guessing.

> Remember that the test instructions require you to record your answer by fully blacking the answer box.

13. The plane is due to depart at 14.15 hours. You are required to check in one and a half hours before departure and need to allow two hours to travel to the airport. What time would you need to leave your house?

A	B	C	D	E	F
11.5	9.45	10.45	Noon	11.45	10.15

14. In the year 1995, 60 per cent of graduates were found to be poor at the interpretation of information when it was presented numerically. If there were 2,200 graduates that year, how many were able to interpret this kind of information?

A	B	C	D	E	F
1320	1100	2200	1400	880	1000

15. A factory worker worked 37½ hours a week. How many hours did she work over a 12-week period?

A	B	C	D	E	F
450	300	444	296	375	950

16. An office worker was required to keep a time sheet detailing how long it took to undertake each task. Excluding lunch, what was the total time taken to complete all the following tasks:

Franking mail	20 minutes
Amending computer files	45 minutes
Answering the telephone	70 minutes
Lunch	30 minutes

A	B	C	D	E	F
2½ hours	2 hours 5 mins	2 hours	1 ¾ hours	2¼ hours	1½ hours

17. A survey in a café found that a quarter of all customers took sugar and an eighth took sweetener. What fraction of customers took no sugar or sweetener?

A	B	C	D	E	F
3/5	9/16	3/8	5/8	1/2	120

18. A survey found that 3/16ths of women said that they would always shop at a complex which offered baby changing facilities. 5/8ths said that they thought it advantageous if a complex offered this service, while the remaining 75 respondents indicated that they thought it made no difference. What number of women said they thought the service advantageous?

A	B	C	D	E	F
25	250	150	50	125	175

19. If a machine is designed to rotate 300 times a minute how many rotations does it perform in an hour?

A	B	C	D	E	F
18 million	9,000	9 million	180,000	18,000	90,000

20. If the fastest student in the class can type at 30 words a minute, while the slowest can only manage 20 words, what would be the time difference between them if they undertook to input a document comprising 3,000 words?

A	B	C	D	E	F
50 minutes	1 hour	45 minutes	1¼ hours	90 minutes	100 minutes

21. An architect designed a long, sweeping staircase which was a total of 16 metres in length. He specified that the staircase was to have 48 steps. Approximately, what was the length of each step?

A	B	C	D	E	F
½ metre	200 cm	¼ metre	300 cm	400 cm	⅓ metre

22. It was recommended that the photocopier was serviced every half a million copies and on average it was used to undertake 70,000 copies a month. How many months should pass between services?

A	B	C	D	E	F
3	8	6	7	9	4

23. The head teacher of a school realised that he had overspent on the wages by 5 per cent. If the monthly total was supposed to be kept under £21,000, how much had been overspent?

A	B	C	D	E	F
£1,500	£950	£1,050	£1,175	£1,000	£700

24. A ship's engine was found to achieve a speed of 9 knots at 2,700 revolutions. How many extra revolutions would you expect to be required if the captain asked to increase the speed to 9.5 knots?

A	B	C	D	E	F
600	400	300	150	450	200

25. Your office used 16 first class stamps at 25 pence and 42 second class stamps at 19 pence. What was the total postage bill?

A	B	C	D	E	F
£13.73	£11.98	£13.29	£11.60	£13.54	£11.73

26. Your office referred 22 files to storage over a three-month period and they took up just over 4 metres of shelving. At this rate how long would you expect it to take before your stored files occupied a kilometre of shelf space (answers are expressed in whole years)?

A	B	C	D	E	F
12 years	10 years	62 years	90 years	83 years	50 years

27. From what time should you book the conference room if the delegates' train arrives at 13.00 hours, the station is approximately 15 minutes away and you expect them to lunch with the minister for two hours before the seminar begins?

A	B	C	D	E	F
Noon	4.00pm	1.30pm	3.15pm	2.00pm	2.45pm

28. The photocopier operates at 45 copies a minute. How many minutes will it take to duplicate 1,100 copies?

A	B	C	D	E	F
20	50	21	55	24	19

29. Three offices decided to share equally the cost of a new piece of equipment. The bill totalled £3,780. How much did each department have to contribute?

A	B	C	D	E	F
£1,260	£260	£2,260	£1,890	£2,890	£890

30. A metre of rope cost 29 pence. How much would 120 metres cost?

A	B	C	D	E	F
£29.29	£36.50	£34.80	£37.10	£29.10	£29.00

31. If 350 people entered a competition and each paid £1.20, how much would remain if the organiser has spent a total of £200 on prizes?

A	B	C	D	E	F
£220.20	£220	£22.40	£218.80	£217.60	215.20

32. A pack of 8 pots of liquid correction fluid costs £7.68. What is the cost of each pot?

A	B	C	D	E	F
130p	85p	76.3p	109p	18p	96p

33. Most telephone calls were received between 10.00 and 11.00 am, which is three times as many as the 150 calls received between 3.00 and 4.00 pm. On average, how many calls a minute were received during the busiest hour?

A	B	C	D	E	F
6	150	7½	2½	16	450

34. A 50-gram item costs 25 pence to post. At the same rate, how much would you expect to pay to post an item that weighted a kilo?

A	B	C	D	E	F
£15	£150	£200	£500	£20	£5

35. If tax on a £150 television set is £22.50, how much tax is paid on a television which costs £1,050?

A	B	C	D	E	F
£157.50	£210.00	£183.75	£105.00	£73.50	£52.50

Sub-test 3. Speed and accuracy

The RAS sub-test 'Speed and Accuracy' requires you to compare sets of numbers or letters arranged in pairs, one on the left the other on the right. Each question comprises four pairs and you have to indicate how many of them are identical. You are offered five possible answers: all four (are identical), three pairs, two pairs, one pair or none.

In the real test you must try to complete 26 questions in 5 minutes, just over 14 seconds a question, so you must work as quickly as possible. Try the following practice questions. Set yourself the first and last 10 questions as practice exams. In each case allow yourself 1 minute 14 seconds!

1. 45981   45981
       xsbaa   xssaa
       kiyhq   kiyhq
       21213   21213

All 4	3 pairs	2 pairs	1 pair	None
☐	☐	☐	☐	☐

2. qwdfk   wqdfk
    33601   33611
    15380   15580
    50179   97150

All 4	3 pairs	2 pairs	1 pair	None

3. hjwep   hjwep
    ffthm   ftthm
    abelo   abelo
    mwwgr   mmwgr

All 4	3 pairs	2 pairs	1 pair	None

4. 58392   53892
    dmhmi   dmdmi
    bdbdv   dbdbv
    illia   ilila

All 4	3 pairs	2 pairs	1 pair	None

5. zxasw   zxasw
    74893   74893
    17204   12704
    01010   01020

All 4	3 pairs	2 pairs	1 pair	None

6. bgdth   gbdth
    zakiv   zakii
    45000   54001
    45001   45000

All 4	3 pairs	2 pairs	1 pair	None

7. sopme   soome
    soppq   soppq
    04517   04518
    49872   49872

All 4	3 pairs	2 pairs	1 pair	None
☐	☐	☐	☐	☐

8. mmhhi   mmhhh
    99933   33399
    fffrr   fffrr
    nhqir   nhqir

All 4	3 pairs	2 pairs	1 pair	None
☐	☐	☐	☐	☐

9. nxruy   nxruy
    qqasw   qqasw
    93462   93462
    ntyue   nteyu

All 4	3 pairs	2 pairs	1 pair	None
☐	☐	☐	☐	☐

10. 15795   15795
    48957   48957
    25846   25864
    35745   35754

All 4	3 pairs	2 pairs	1 pair	None
☐	☐	☐	☐	☐

11. ilop   kliop
    kopli   kploi
    poilk   polik
    oolip   ollip

All 4	3 pairs	2 pairs	1 pair	None
☐	☐	☐	☐	☐

12. vfrtg   fgtrv
     gfrtv   gfrtv
     frtgv   frtgv
     gfrtf   rtfgt

All 4	3 pairs	2 pairs	1 pair	None
☐	☐	☐	☐	☐

13. 20250   25052
     0425   0425
     65658   65658
     20052   20052

All 4	3 pairs	2 pairs	1 pair	None
☐	☐	☐	☐	☐

14. blgos   blgos
     werqw   werqw
     14584   14584
     36526   36526

All 4	3 pairs	2 pairs	1 pair	None
☐	☐	☐	☐	☐

15. 07078   07078
     asdfg   asdfg
     gfdsa   gfdsa
     03256   03256

All 4	3 pairs	2 pairs	1 pair	None
☐	☐	☐	☐	☐

16. wuyoi   wuyoi
     30057   30057
     dflkk   dflkk
     45008   45008

All 4	3 pairs	2 pairs	1 pair	None
☐	☐	☐	☐	☐

17. 49057   49057
     00558   00558
     asiore   asoire
     nheppo   nheppo

All 4	3 pairs	2 pairs	1 pair	None

18. 4584584   4584584
     32658   32658
     500505   500505
     054585   0548458

All 4	3 pairs	2 pairs	1 pair	None

19. gpr ty   gprty
     druowff   druuowff
     foluaw   foluaw
     brtrt   brtrt

All 4	3 pairs	2 pairs	1 pair	None

20. 137946   137946
     438679   438679
     402794   4022794
     4586003   4586603

All 4	3 pairs	2 pairs	1 pair	None

21. df er ty s   df er ty s
     fgtyuoi   fgtyuoi
     cdf gtyg   cdfgtyy
     mmyyeeq   mmyyyeeq

All 4	3 pairs	2 pairs	1 pair	None

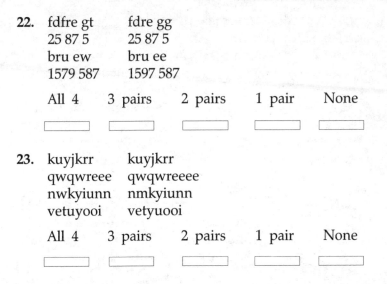

22. fdfre gt   fdre gg
25 87 5   25 87 5
bru ew   bru ee
1579 587   1597 587

All 4   3 pairs   2 pairs   1 pair   None

23. kuyjkrr   kuyjkrr
qwqwreee   qwqwreeee
nwkyiunn   nmkyiunn
vetuyooi   vetyuooi

All 4   3 pairs   2 pairs   1 pair   None

These questions are very easy to make up. If you feel you need more practice, why not create some more yourself?

Sub-test 4. Composite test

You are allowed 6 minutes in which to attempt 9 questions in the real composite test and are required to read a passage and, using the information it contains, decide if the statements listed are either true or false.

Each question consists of two statements labelled A and B. This means that there are four possible answers to all the questions namely: both statements are true, both statements are false, statement A is true while B is false or B is true while A is false. Your task is to establish which of these situations applies and mark the appropriate box.

Try the following practice questions. It helps to read the statements before you read the passage.

Passage 1
Mrs Brewer, the office manager, was charged with responsibility for replacing the existing photocopier. The specifications were to remain the same in that the machine was to be able to make 50,000 copies a month, operate at least at 40 copies a minute, have the facility for double-sided copying, a feed tray and sorter bin. She was told that she could con-

sider ex-demonstration or new machines but must not purchase a service agreement.

Mrs Brewer embarked on the task with some apprehension as she was well aware of the bad reputation of photocopier sales staff. She decided to write out a list of specifications and sent this to a number of companies requesting written quotations and details of their products. Soon afterwards she started to receive calls from the company representatives offering her all kinds of deals.

Questions

1. Statement: A   Mrs Brewer requested that the sales representatives telephone her.
              B   She wanted a machine which could handle double-sided copying.

A CORRECT	A CORRECT	A INCORRECT	A INCORRECT
B CORRECT	B INCORRECT	B CORRECT	B INCORRECT
☐	☐	☐	☐

2. Statement A   A service agreement was to be part of the deal.
             B   More features were required of the new machine.

A CORRECT	A CORRECT	A INCORRECT	A INCORRECT
B CORRECT	B INCORRECT	B CORRECT	B INCORRECT
☐	☐	☐	☐

3. Statement A   Mrs Brewer requires the sales representatives to send her two types of information.
             B   She has a preference for a new machine rather than one that has been reconditioned.

A CORRECT	A CORRECT	A INCORRECT	A INCORRECT
B CORRECT	B INCORRECT	B CORRECT	B INCORRECT
☐	☐	☐	☐

4. Statement   A   While she was apprehensive, Mrs Brewer was able to take some consolation from the fact that she was not solely responsible for the decision over which copier to purchase.

    B   Photocopier sales staff have a reputation.

A CORRECT	A CORRECT	A INCORRECT	A INCORRECT
B CORRECT	B INCORRECT	B CORRECT	B INCORRECT

[ ]	[ ]	[ ]	[ ]

5. Statement   A   Mrs Brewer's copier would need to undertake over half a million copies a year.

    B   A machine which could undertake just under 2,000 copies an hour would not meet her specification.

A CORRECT	A CORRECT	A INCORRECT	A INCORRECT
B CORRECT	B INCORRECT	B CORRECT	B INCORRECT

[ ]	[ ]	[ ]	[ ]

Passage 2

Mr Waters, a tool-maker with Johnson and Matthew, left his machine to record in the company's accident book the fact that he had received a small splinter of steel in his thumb. This was a common accident for someone in his trade and he knew the company nurse would have to remove it, otherwise it was likely to become infected.

As he wrote down the circumstances of his accident he noticed a leaflet which read: 'The Health and Safety at Work Act is aimed at securing the health, safety and welfare of all workers. It requires employers to ensure the safety of their employees at work but also places a legal responsibility on every individual, whilst at work, to take care of their own and their colleagues' health and safety. Workers must cooperate with their employers to ensure that their place of work is safe. The Act allows that both employers and employees can be fined or sent to prison if they fail to fulfil their legal duties. In large organisations health and safety representatives are elected to represent the workers and to carry out safety checks.'

Questions

6.   Statement   A   The Act requires every individual to take care to avoid injury to themselves.

B   Mr Waters has a legal duty to consider the safety of his fellow workers.

A CORRECT	A CORRECT	A INCORRECT	A INCORRECT
B CORRECT	B INCORRECT	B CORRECT	B INCORRECT
☐	☐	☐	☐

7.   Statement   A   The Act requires all employers to have safety representatives.

B   Mr Waters read that he would receive compensation for his injury.

A CORRECT	A CORRECT	A INCORRECT	A INCORRECT
B CORRECT	B INCORRECT	B CORRECT	B INCORRECT
☐	☐	☐	☐

8.   Statement   A   Mr Waters' employers risked imprisonment or a fine if they did not maintain a safe place of work.

B   Mr Waters' thumb required medical attention.

A CORRECT	A CORRECT	A INCORRECT	A INCORRECT
B CORRECT	B INCORRECT	B CORRECT	B INCORRECT
☐	☐	☐	☐

9. Statement   A   Mr Waters is required to record the circumstances of the accident in the accident book.

   B   Fortunately, the book was kept beside Mr Waters' machine.

A CORRECT	A CORRECT	A INCORRECT	A INCORRECT
B CORRECT	B INCORRECT	B CORRECT	B INCORRECT
⬜	⬜	⬜	⬜

10. Statement   A   The company provided a written explanation of the Health and Safety at Work Act.

   B   Splinters of metal were an occupational hazard for tool-makers.

A CORRECT	A CORRECT	A INCORRECT	A INCORRECT
B CORRECT	B INCORRECT	B CORRECT	B INCORRECT
⬜	⬜	⬜	⬜

Answers to practice exercises

Following procedures (page 39)

1   B
2   E
3   E
4   D
5   E, G, H
6   D
7   G, H
8   F
9   E, F, I
10   D

Numerical tasks (page 42)

1   920.1
2   3.6
3   1736

4   1.024
5   210
6   1¾
7   166.4
8   50%
9   600
10   135
11   133⅓
12   6,000
13   C
14   E
15   A
16   E
17   D
18   B
19   E
20   A
21   F
22   D
23   C
24   D
25   B
26   C
27   D
28   E
29   A
30   C
31   B
32   F
33   C
34   F
35   A

Speed and accuracy (page 48)
1   3 pairs
2   None
3   2 pairs
4   None
5   2 pairs
6   None

7	2 pairs
8	2 pairs
9	3 pairs
10	2 pairs
11	None
12	2 pairs
13	3 pairs
14	all 4
15	all 4
16	all 4
17	3 pairs
18	3 pairs
19	2 pairs
20	2 pairs
21	2 pairs
22	1 pair
23	1 pair

Composite test (page 53)

1	A incorrect B correct
2	A incorrect B incorrect
3	A correct B incorrect
4	A incorrect B correct
5	A correct B correct
6	A correct B correct
7	A incorrect B incorrect
8	A correct B correct
9	A correct B incorrect
10	A correct B correct

If you suffer a disability which might affect your test performance telephone the RAS or the Personnel section of the Department and discuss it with them prior to the test day.

Chapter 4

Practice for the Executive Officer Qualifying Test

The RAS Executive Officer qualifying test

The Executive Officer qualifying test typically comprises four sub-tests which are administered in one session. This means that you take all four consecutively without a break.

All candidates invited to sit the tests are sent a description and a few examples of the types of question. RAS believe that by studying the description and practising on the example questions candidates will have a better understanding of what is required of them. The cost of sending out material means that RAS must restrict the amount of practice material they can provide. It is intended that this book will help to make up any shortfall.

In the real tests you may find that you do not have sufficient time to complete all the questions and that the questions get increasingly more difficult. You are not allowed to use a calculator, computer, slide rule or any other type of aid.

It is important for you to realise that the qualifying test exists in two formats. Some of you will take a paper and pencil version while others will take the test on a computer. Your invitation will inform you which version you face. The principal difference is the way in which you enter your answers. In both cases the test is designed so that large numbers of papers can be marked mechanically.

In the case of the paper and pencil version you are required to make a bold mark with the pencil in the answer box. If you decide to change your answer or make a mistake it is important that you thoroughly erase your first answer. You are asked to bring along your own pencil and eraser.

Those of you who take the test on the computer terminal can page backwards or forwards by moving the cursor (or what RAS call the arrow) and enter your answers with a keyboard. In either case, full instructions are given before you start the tests and are repeated prior to each of the sub-tests.

Whichever version of the test you take it is important to work as quickly as you can and not to spend too long on any one question. If you cannot answer a question promptly then move on to the next one and return later if you have time. Avoid rushing as this causes unnecessary mistakes.

In the remainder of this chapter questions are provided for each of the four sub-test types, with answers provided at the end of the chapter.

Practice exercises

Sentence sequence

The real RAS sentence sequence sub-test comprises 26 passages, each four sentences long. The sentences are numbered, but the order in which they were originally written has been lost and the sentences are now in the wrong order. Your task is to put the sentences into the correct order. RAS define the correct order as 'the way the writer originally wrote them'.

You are allowed 22 minutes to reorganise the 26 passages. This means that you have on average just over 50 seconds per passage. The passages will get increasingly complex so you should complete the opening passages in less time than this. With practice some candidates show a considerable improvement in this type of exercise.

Below you will find practice questions and a mock test. I have adopted the style of answer box used in the paper and pencil version of the test. To indicate your answer, draw a bold, solid horizontal line across each column in the answer box. I have completed the first example so that you can see how.

I am indebted to Ian Whittaker for devising many of these practice sentences.

Example question

1. As he moved towards the stove he picked up the oven glove.
2. He took care to make sure that the steam would not scald him and he turned off the gas.
3. James looked up from the paper to notice that the kettle was boiling furiously.
4. He poured the water into the teapot successfully.

1[ ]	1[⊢⊣]	1[ ]	1[ ]
2[ ]	2[ ]	2[⊢⊣]	2[ ]
3[⊢⊣]	3[ ]	3[ ]	3[ ]
4[ ]	4[ ]	4[ ]	4[⊢⊣]

Correct order 3, 1, 2, 4.

Practice questions

1. 1. Put out your arm when you see the bus coming.
2. Tender the correct change to the conductor.
3. Climb in.
4. Tell her where you want to alight.

1[ ]	1[ ]	1[ ]	1[ ]
2[ ]	2[ ]	2[ ]	2[ ]
3[ ]	3[ ]	3[ ]	3[ ]
4[ ]	4[ ]	4[ ]	4[ ]

2. 1. The engine roared into life.
2. The '57 Chevy careered dangerously into the sunset.
3. There was a stomach-churning grating of gears.
4. The tyres squealed as it pulled away.

1[ ]	1[ ]	1[ ]	1[ ]
2[ ]	2[ ]	2[ ]	2[ ]
3[ ]	3[ ]	3[ ]	3[ ]
4[ ]	4[ ]	4[ ]	4[ ]

3. 1. The medieval period saw a large growth in the construction of cathedrals.
    2. Its main characteristic was parallel stone mullions running the entire height of the windows.
    3. One such was perpendicular Gothic.
    4. They were built in a number of styles.

1[ ]	1[ ]	1[ ]	1[ ]
2[ ]	2[ ]	2[ ]	2[ ]
3[ ]	3[ ]	3[ ]	3[ ]
4[ ]	4[ ]	4[ ]	4[ ]

4. 1. The carrots cascaded from the scale pan into the bag.
    2. The grocer deftly spun it before handing it over.
    3. He pulled a paper bag from the hook.
    4. Mr Benjamin placed it into his shopping bag.

1[ ]	1[ ]	1[ ]	1[ ]
2[ ]	2[ ]	2[ ]	2[ ]
3[ ]	3[ ]	3[ ]	3[ ]
4[ ]	4[ ]	4[ ]	4[ ]

5. 1. He proffered a flaring match.
    2. 'Have you got a light?' came a once-familiar voice.
    3. In its flickering light he recognised her as his former boss.
    4. He tentatively asked 'Is your name Karen Morris?'

1[ ]	1[ ]	1[ ]	1[ ]
2[ ]	2[ ]	2[ ]	2[ ]
3[ ]	3[ ]	3[ ]	3[ ]
4[ ]	4[ ]	4[ ]	4[ ]

6. 1. The former did not reach the South Pole first, but died heroically on his return journey.
    2. There were two Antarctic expeditions in 1912.
    3. The latter, a Norwegian, was the first man to reach the South Pole, but in comparatively unremarkable circumstances.
    4. Arguably, Captain Scott's was more famous than Amundsen's.

1[ ]	1[ ]	1[ ]	1[ ]
2[ ]	2[ ]	2[ ]	2[ ]
3[ ]	3[ ]	3[ ]	3[ ]
4[ ]	4[ ]	4[ ]	4[ ]

7. 1. Having bought the shares the stockbroker transferred them to the client.
    2. Before the Big Bang in 1986 the method of buying shares in the London market was different.
    3. The broker then approached a jobber to buy the shares.
    4. The client would approach a stockbroker.

1[ ]	1[ ]	1[ ]	1[ ]
2[ ]	2[ ]	2[ ]	2[ ]
3[ ]	3[ ]	3[ ]	3[ ]
4[ ]	4[ ]	4[ ]	4[ ]

8. 1. It is so called because being large, slow and buoyant when dead it was the 'right' whale to catch.
    2. The decline has been most pronounced among the larger whales, and scientists fear that a number of species, particularly the right whale, might become extinct.
    3. This century, as fishing methods became more effective, the decline in the whale population occurred very rapidly.

4. Whales are now protected and their numbers are expected to rise.

1[ ]	1[ ]	1[ ]	1[ ]
2[ ]	2[ ]	2[ ]	2[ ]
3[ ]	3[ ]	3[ ]	3[ ]
4[ ]	4[ ]	4[ ]	4[ ]

9. 1. Frantically he tore at the coils around his neck.
    2. Once the bedding was straight, she assured him, 'It's all right, the Doctor's on his way.'
    3. Gently his mother unravelled the sheet and kissed his fevered brow.
    4. The anaconda coiled itself around his body, squeezing the lifeblood from him.

1[ ]	1[ ]	1[ ]	1[ ]
2[ ]	2[ ]	2[ ]	2[ ]
3[ ]	3[ ]	3[ ]	3[ ]
4[ ]	4[ ]	4[ ]	4[ ]

10. 1. The Institute claims to show that executive pay in the 1980s outstripped that on the factory floor.
    2. that Britain's executives are threatening the rate of economic recovery by awarding themselves unwarranted pay rises.
    3. The National Institute of Economic and Social Research has apparently confirmed what many have long suspected:
    4. What is more the study found that executive pay rises in the 1990s have little or no connection with company performance.

1[ ]	1[ ]	1[ ]	1[ ]
2[ ]	2[ ]	2[ ]	2[ ]
3[ ]	3[ ]	3[ ]	3[ ]
4[ ]	4[ ]	4[ ]	4[ ]

11. 1. After the war he served on the cruiser *Jamaica* in the West Indies.

2. The son of a naval engineer, Hugo Janier went to Dartmouth at the age of 13 in 1937.

3. His final post as a captain was in command of the guided-missile destroyer *Bristol*.

4. Graduating during the war, he saw service as a midshipman on the battleship *Rodney*.

1[ ]	1[ ]	1[ ]	1[ ]
2[ ]	2[ ]	2[ ]	2[ ]
3[ ]	3[ ]	3[ ]	3[ ]
4[ ]	4[ ]	4[ ]	4[ ]

12. 1. Having been taken to the police station under arrest, as soon as practicable a decision will be made on whether to press charges.

2. In the Magistrates Court the case will either be disposed of or adjourned to another sitting.

3. The suspect should be legally arrested by a police officer, designated official or citizen.

4. If charged, the suspect will be detained or released on bail to attend the Magistrates Court at a given time on a given day.

1[ ]	1[ ]	1[ ]	1[ ]
2[ ]	2[ ]	2[ ]	2[ ]
3[ ]	3[ ]	3[ ]	3[ ]
4[ ]	4[ ]	4[ ]	4[ ]

13. 1. Alternatively, on a verdict of guilty, the defendant will be sentenced immediately or have the case adjourned for sentence in order to allow a pre-sentence report to be made.

2. At the end of the speeches the judge will sum up the case for the jury, who will then retire in the custody of the jury bailiff to make their deliberations.

3.   Counsel for defence will make her closing speech.
4.   Having given their verdict, the defendant, if she is acquitted, is then free to leave.

1[ ]	1[ ]	1[ ]	1[ ]
2[ ]	2[ ]	2[ ]	2[ ]
3[ ]	3[ ]	3[ ]	3[ ]
4[ ]	4[ ]	4[ ]	4[ ]

14. 1.   The disaster was narrowly avoided and the track man received a medal and a reward for his bravery.
2.   Imperceptibly at first, the train began to roll down the track, picking up speed.
3.   In his eagerness to get clearance from the signalman the train driver climbed down from the cab, forgetting to apply the brakes.
4.   Seeing another train on the tracks and the impending disaster, the track worker threw down his shovel, leapt into the cab and applied the brake.

1[ ]	1[ ]	1[ ]	1[ ]
2[ ]	2[ ]	2[ ]	2[ ]
3[ ]	3[ ]	3[ ]	3[ ]
4[ ]	4[ ]	4[ ]	4[ ]

Data interpretation

You are allowed 41 minutes to complete 29 questions in the real data interpretation RAS sub-test. Note that this test also occurs in the Fast Stream battery. It comprises 10 tables of numerical data with between two and four questions relating to each. It is difficult to estimate how long you should spend on each question because you must interpret the tables first.

The sub-test is a multiple-choice paper with a total of four suggested answers for each question. It may pay to look at the suggested answers prior to attempting lengthy calculations as it is sometimes possible to rule some of them out and to estimate the correct answer by rounding sums up to more convenient figures. If you do not have sufficient time to finish, try an educated guess.

Each suggested answer is given a number. To record your answer you simply mark the number in the answer box.

Practice questions

Table 1
The table below indicates the total number of young people and what they did after leaving school in the rural districts of an English county between the years 1988–91.

Year	1988	1989	1990	1991
No of school leavers	3000	2196	2400	1652
Returned to education	450	769	480	798
Entered employment	300	285	240	189
Entered training	600	483	480	266
Unemployed	750	373	480	147
Left district	150	66	120	189
Unknown	750	220	600	63

1. Between the years 1988 and 1990, which after-school activity saw the greatest percentage increase?

   1) returned to education   2) entered training   3) became unemployed   4) left district

1	2	3	4
[ ]	[ ]	[ ]	[ ]

2. How many activities were selected by the same percentage of young people in 1988 and 1990?

   1) two categories   2) four categories   3) five categories   4) three categories

1	2	3	4
[ ]	[ ]	[ ]	[ ]

3.   How many more times popular was returning to education compared with entering training in 1991?

1) five times   2) six times   3) four times   4) three times

1	2	3	4
[ ]	[ ]	[ ]	[ ]

4.   Over the four-year period what was the average number of annual school leavers?

1) 2309   2) 3216   3) 2312   4) 0238

1	2	3	4
[ ]	[ ]	[ ]	[ ]

Table 2
The table below illustrates the population structure of five countries. The data relates to January 1990.

Country	Total population (millions)	Live births per 1,000	Deaths per 1,000
Country A	56.4	13.2	11.9
Country B	53.6	12.9	12.3
Country C	70.3	11.7	11.6
Country D	12.7	9.9	10.1
Country E	18.2	10.8	11.2

5.   Which country is experiencing the fastest rate of growth in population?

1) A   2) B   3) C   4) E

1	2	3	4
[ ]	[ ]	[ ]	[ ]

6. Which country's population is over four times smaller than country B's?

    1) A   2) B   3) C   4) D

1	2	3	4
[ ]	[ ]	[ ]	[ ]

7. Which country experienced just over 125,000 births?

    1) B   2) C   3) D   4) E

1	2	3	4
[ ]	[ ]	[ ]	[ ]

8. Which two countries experienced a mean rate of death per thousand of 11.55?

    1) A and B   2) A and E   3) A and C   4) D and E

1	2	3	4
[ ]	[ ]	[ ]	[ ]

Table 3

The table below shows the monthly average rainfall, hours of sunshine and wind speed for a European country. Consult it to answer the questions below.

	Rainfall (mm)	Sunshine (hours)	Wind speed (knots)
January	91	54	21
February	108	80	17
March	155	140	15
April	160	153	13
May	121	165	12
June	97	228	9
July	78	218	10
August	80	200	11
September	113	193	12

	Rainfall (mm)	Sunshine (hours)	Wind speed (knots)
October	102	120	15
November	114	90	16
December	103	64	18

9.   What is the mean wind speed for the months of January, February and March?

   1) 18.11   2) 16.66   3) 17.66   4) 15.33

```
   1      2      3      4
 [ ]    [ ]    [ ]    [ ]
```

10. Which three consecutive months have a total of 403 hours of sunshine?

   1) May, June, July   2) October, November, December
   2) March, April, May   4) September, October, November

```
   1      2      3      4
 [ ]    [ ]    [ ]    [ ]
```

11. Identify the percentage which expresses the increase in sunshine between the months of February and March.

   1) 75%   2) 8%   3) 16%   4) 50%

```
   1      2      3      4
 [ ]    [ ]    [ ]    [ ]
```

12. What is the ratio between the rainfall during the wettest and driest months?

   1) 2:1   2) 1:2   3) 1:3   4) 3:1

```
   1      2      3      4
 [ ]    [ ]    [ ]    [ ]
```

Word link

The real word link sub-test comprises 35 questions for which you are allowed 15½ minutes. This means that you must complete each question in under 30 seconds.

The questions comprise two lines of words, one above the other. On the top line are two words, while on the lower there are six. RAS describe what you must do as: 'Your task is to identify two words in the lower line, one in each half, which forms an analogy when paired with the word in the upper line.' You indicate your answer by underlining the two words on the lower line. Although an analogy is when the words are in some way similar, note that in some questions the connection between the words is that they are opposites.

Again I am grateful for the assistance of Ian Whittaker.

Example questions
1.   FLAT   ROUGH
     <u>even</u> Taxidermist hatchback   mouse house <u>rugged</u>

The connection in this case is that the words are opposites.

2.   FAST   FEAST
     conversion rapid <u>diet</u>   <u>slow</u> gluttony waterfall

The connection is that the opposite of 'fast' is 'slow' and the opposite of 'feast' is 'diet' but note how the connections are made diagonally across the top and bottom line.

3.   HORSE   CAR
Putter <u>rider</u> jump   pig <u>driver</u> cow

The connection in this example is that a horse has a rider and a car a driver.

Practice questions
1.   CRICKET   BAT
     golf locust vampire   grasshopper club grass

2.   SAILOR   SURGEON
     hornpipe ship trumpet   xylophone hospital waltz

3. RUN   CONTROL
    sprint manage trot   walk regulate relax

4. HIGH   LOW
    intoxicated top above   buttock bottom beyond

5. CLOWN   CIRCUS
    idiot king approximate   roundabout palace pin

6. ASSEMBLE   WITHDRAW
    enjoy construct retreat   age retire superannuate

7. JUDGE   JOCKEY
    date court horse   bench club isotherm

8. CONCUR   ARGUE
    agree reject explain   propose dispute believe

9. KING   KINGDOM
    kong emperor size   empire penguin hall

10. RABBIT   FUR
    hearse horse hoarse   hair hare heir

11. YACHT   SAIL
    care car dinghy   truck engine outboard

12. DAWN   SUNSET
    patrol stars light   moon boulevard dark

13. GOVERNMENT   CHAOS
    free anarchy conservative   liberal order command

14. SOCIALIST   ENVIRONMENTALIST
    red blue black   yellow white green

15. CHINA   FRANCE
    clay tea Asia   polish wine Europe

16. INEPT   PERFECT
    complete apt competent   whole exodus defective

17. DRAWS   ASSESSES
    sketch sledge attractions   praises amalgamate appraises

Number sequences

Thirty-one questions make up this sub-test of the Executive Officer battery and you have on average just over 30 seconds for each and 17 minutes in total.

Each question contains a sequence of numbers but one set is missing and has been replaced with the letters 'XX'. You are required to identify the missing numbers and complete the answer box accordingly. In most cases it is a pair of numbers which are missing. However, if the answer is a single digit then make sure you prefix your answer with a zero. For example, to indicate the single digit 5 as the answer, mark the answer box to read '05'.

For many candidates sequencing tests offer the chance to show considerable improvement through practice. They really are a lot easier than they at first seem. If you are unfamiliar with this type of question you will find it of benefit to learn the most common types of sequence on which the questions are based.

I owe particular thanks to Bruce Bush for helping to devise these number sequence questions and identifying the most common types.

The most common types of numerical sequences

Addition
This is one of the most common types of sequence. To get the sequence you simply add the same number to the previous term each time. For example, the sequence obtained from addition of the number 3 is as follows:

    2 5 8 11 14 17 20 23 26 29 and so on.

A sequence can start from any point. For example, the sequence arrived at from adding the number 8 can be presented as follows:

480 488 496 504 512 520 528 536 and so on.

Subtraction
If a sequence is decreasing from the left it may be that it is the result of subtraction. A sequence which results from the subtraction of the figure 6 can be illustrated as follows:

540 534 528 522 516 510 504 498 492 486 480

Multiplication
These common types of sequence are constructed as a result of multiplying by the same number each time. For example, the sequence derived by the multiplication of 3 each time is as follows:

2 6 18 54 162 486

Division
In a way similar to multiplication, a sequence can be constructed as a result of division by the same number each time. For example, division by 5 each time produces the following sequence:

37,500 7,500 1,500 300 60

Add two previous terms
This type of sequence is generated by adding the two previous numbers to obtain the next in the series. We take the first two numbers as given. For example:

1 4 5 9 14 23 37

In this case we have obtained 5 by adding 1 + 4, the two previous numbers, and 4 + 9 to obtain 14 and so on.

Multiply two previous numbers
Related to the previous example of addition of two previous numbers, this sequence is obtained by multiplication of the two previous digits. For example:

3 4 12 48 576

$3 \times 4 = 12, 4 \times 12 = 48, 12 \times 48 = 576$

Alternating signs

A number may have either a positive or negative sign and the sign of the numbers which make up a sequence may be alternated in an attempt to make it less recognisable. An example of an alternative sign sequence is:

$$2 - 4 \ \ 8 - 16 \ \ 32 - 64 \ \ 128$$

Addition of two common sequences

These sequences are produced as a result of adding a number to the first term to get the second but adding a different number to get the third and a different number again to get the fourth, and so on. You can work out which number to add each time because they belong to another sequence. To illustrate the point take the sequence:

$$1 \ 2 \ 4 \ 7 \ 11 \ 16 \ 22 \ 29 \ 37 \ 46$$

It is produced by adding a term from the sequence 1 2 3 4 5 6 7 8 9 to the previous number. For example, to get 2 we add 1 to the previous term, to get 4 we add 2 to the previous term, to get 7 we add 3 to the previous term and so on.

Hidden series

Sometimes the test author will try to hide a sequence by presenting the numbers in a misleading manner. For example:

$$123 \ \ 456 \ \ 789 \ \ 101 \ \ 112 \ \ 131 \ \ 415 \ \ 161 \ \ 718$$

All the test author has done in this instance is present the most common sequence of all in a different way. The sequence is the numbers 1 to 18.

Superimposed sequences

Towards the end of a test the sequences get harder and a common type employed often involves the combining of two well-known sequences. In these sorts the 1st, 3rd, 5th, 7th etc terms may belong to one sequence while the 2nd, 4th, 6th, 8th etc belong to another. An illustration of this kind of sequence is as follows:

$$1 \ 2 \ 4 \ 4 \ 9 \ 8 \ 16 \ 16 \ 25 \ 32 \ 36 \ 64$$

This sequence is made up by combining the following two common sequences:

1 4 9 16 25 36

2 4 8 16 32 64

Sequences worth remembering
A few sequences come up time and time again and if you are unfamiliar with them it is worth committing them to memory.

The power of 2 sequence	2 4 8 16 32 64 128 256
The power of 3 sequence	3 9 27 81 243 729
The squares of numbers	1 4 9 16 25 36 49 64 81 100
A sequence of factors	1 2 6 24 120 720
The cubes of numbers	1 8 27 64 125 216
The power of 4 sequence	4 16 64 256 1024
The sequence of prime numbers	1 2 3 5 7 11 13 17 19 23 29

Practice questions
1. 20 33 46 XX 72

0[ ]	0[ ]
1[ ]	1[ ]
2[ ]	2[ ]
3[ ]	3[ ]
4[ ]	4[ ]
5[ ]	5[ ]
6[ ]	6[ ]
7[ ]	7[ ]
8[ ]	8[ ]
9[ ]	9[ ]

2.   6   9   XX   15   18

0[ ]	0[ ]
1[ ]	1[ ]
2[ ]	2[ ]
3[ ]	3[ ]
4[ ]	4[ ]
5[ ]	5[ ]
6[ ]	6[ ]
7[ ]	7[ ]
8[ ]	8[ ]
9[ ]	9[ ]

3.   61   122   183   2XX   305

0[ ]	0[ ]
1[ ]	1[ ]
2[ ]	2[ ]
3[ ]	3[ ]
4[ ]	4[ ]
5[ ]	5[ ]
6[ ]	6[ ]
7[ ]	7[ ]
8[ ]	8[ ]
9[ ]	9[ ]

4.   1027   963   8XX   835

0[ ]	0[ ]
1[ ]	1[ ]
2[ ]	2[ ]
3[ ]	3[ ]
4[ ]	4[ ]
5[ ]	5[ ]
6[ ]	6[ ]
7[ ]	7[ ]
8[ ]	8[ ]
9[ ]	9[ ]

5.   5   10   20   XX   80

```
0[ ]    0[ ]
1[ ]    1[ ]
2[ ]    2[ ]
3[ ]    3[ ]
4[ ]    4[ ]
5[ ]    5[ ]
6[ ]    6[ ]
7[ ]    7[ ]
8[ ]    8[ ]
9[ ]    9[ ]
```

6.   3   12   48   1XX   768

```
0[ ]    0[ ]
1[ ]    1[ ]
2[ ]    2[ ]
3[ ]    3[ ]
4[ ]    4[ ]
5[ ]    5[ ]
6[ ]    6[ ]
7[ ]    7[ ]
8[ ]    8[ ]
9[ ]    9[ ]
```

7.   2   6   18   54   1XX

```
0[ ]    0[ ]
1[ ]    1[ ]
2[ ]    2[ ]
3[ ]    3[ ]
4[ ]    4[ ]
5[ ]    5[ ]
6[ ]    6[ ]
7[ ]    7[ ]
8[ ]    8[ ]
9[ ]    9[ ]
```

8.   3   5   7   XX   13   15

```
0[ ]    0[ ]
1[ ]    1[ ]
2[ ]    2[ ]
3[ ]    3[ ]
4[ ]    4[ ]
5[ ]    5[ ]
6[ ]    6[ ]
7[ ]    7[ ]
8[ ]    8[ ]
9[ ]    9[ ]
```

9.   64   32   16   XX   4   2   1

```
0[ ]    0[ ]
1[ ]    1[ ]
2[ ]    2[ ]
3[ ]    3[ ]
4[ ]    4[ ]
5[ ]    5[ ]
6[ ]    6[ ]
7[ ]    7[ ]
8[ ]    8[ ]
9[ ]    9[ ]
```

10.   4   6   8   XX   12   14   16

```
0[ ]    0[ ]
1[ ]    1[ ]
2[ ]    2[ ]
3[ ]    3[ ]
4[ ]    4[ ]
5[ ]    5[ ]
6[ ]    6[ ]
7[ ]    7[ ]
8[ ]    8[ ]
9[ ]    9[ ]
```

11. 20 18 16 14 XX 14 16 18 20

0[ ]	0[ ]
1[ ]	1[ ]
2[ ]	2[ ]
3[ ]	3[ ]
4[ ]	4[ ]
5[ ]	5[ ]
6[ ]	6[ ]
7[ ]	7[ ]
8[ ]	8[ ]
9[ ]	9[ ]

12. 2 3 5 6 XX 9 11 12 14

0[ ]	0[ ]
1[ ]	1[ ]
2[ ]	2[ ]
3[ ]	3[ ]
4[ ]	4[ ]
5[ ]	5[ ]
6[ ]	6[ ]
7[ ]	7[ ]
8[ ]	8[ ]
9[ ]	9[ ]

13. 5 7 10 14 XX 25 32 40

0[ ]	0[ ]
1[ ]	1[ ]
2[ ]	2[ ]
3[ ]	3[ ]
4[ ]	4[ ]
5[ ]	5[ ]
6[ ]	6[ ]
7[ ]	7[ ]
8[ ]	8[ ]
9[ ]	9[ ]

14.   23   20   17   XX   11   8   5

0[ ]	0[ ]
1[ ]	1[ ]
2[ ]	2[ ]
3[ ]	3[ ]
4[ ]	4[ ]
5[ ]	5[ ]
6[ ]	6[ ]
7[ ]	7[ ]
8[ ]	8[ ]
9[ ]	9[ ]

15.   ½   ¼   ¾   1 $^7/_4$ $^{XX}/_4$

0[ ]	0[ ]
1[ ]	1[ ]
2[ ]	2[ ]
3[ ]	3[ ]
4[ ]	4[ ]
5[ ]	5[ ]
6[ ]	6[ ]
7[ ]	7[ ]
8[ ]	8[ ]
9[ ]	9[ ]

16.   121   36   157   193   3XX

0[ ]	0[ ]
1[ ]	1[ ]
2[ ]	2[ ]
3[ ]	3[ ]
4[ ]	4[ ]
5[ ]	5[ ]
6[ ]	6[ ]
7[ ]	7[ ]
8[ ]	8[ ]
9[ ]	9[ ]

17. 100 1 101 102 XX3

0[ ] 0[ ]
1[ ] 1[ ]
2[ ] 2[ ]
3[ ] 3[ ]
4[ ] 4[ ]
5[ ] 5[ ]
6[ ] 6[ ]
7[ ] 7[ ]
8[ ] 8[ ]
9[ ] 9[ ]

18. 5 2 10 20 200 XX00

0[ ] 0[ ]
1[ ] 1[ ]
2[ ] 2[ ]
3[ ] 3[ ]
4[ ] 4[ ]
5[ ] 5[ ]
6[ ] 6[ ]
7[ ] 7[ ]
8[ ] 8[ ]
9[ ] 9[ ]

19. 12 −24 36 − 48 XX

0[ ] 0[ ]
1[ ] 1[ ]
2[ ] 2[ ]
3[ ] 3[ ]
4[ ] 4[ ]
5[ ] 5[ ]
6[ ] 6[ ]
7[ ] 7[ ]
8[ ] 8[ ]
9[ ] 9[ ]

20.   42   −33   24   −15   XX

0[ ]	0[ ]
1[ ]	1[ ]
2[ ]	2[ ]
3[ ]	3[ ]
4[ ]	4[ ]
5[ ]	5[ ]
6[ ]	6[ ]
7[ ]	7[ ]
8[ ]	8[ ]
9[ ]	9[ ]

21.   12   XX   −8   −6   4   2

0[ ]	0[ ]
1[ ]	1[ ]
2[ ]	2[ ]
3[ ]	3[ ]
4[ ]	4[ ]
5[ ]	5[ ]
6[ ]	6[ ]
7[ ]	7[ ]
8[ ]	8[ ]
9[ ]	9[ ]

22.   2   −¼   6   −⅛   XX

0[ ]	0[ ]
1[ ]	1[ ]
2[ ]	2[ ]
3[ ]	3[ ]
4[ ]	4[ ]
5[ ]	5[ ]
6[ ]	6[ ]
7[ ]	7[ ]
8[ ]	8[ ]
9[ ]	9[ ]

23. 1   3   7   15   XX

```
0[  ]    0[  ]
1[  ]    1[  ]
2[  ]    2[  ]
3[  ]    3[  ]
4[  ]    4[  ]
5[  ]    5[  ]
6[  ]    6[  ]
7[  ]    7[  ]
8[  ]    8[  ]
9[  ]    9[  ]
```

24. 1 $\frac{1}{3}$ 9 $\frac{1}{27}$ XX

```
0[  ]    0[  ]
1[  ]    1[  ]
2[  ]    2[  ]
3[  ]    3[  ]
4[  ]    4[  ]
5[  ]    5[  ]
6[  ]    6[  ]
7[  ]    7[  ]
8[  ]    8[  ]
9[  ]    9[  ]
```

25. 4   5   10   28   82   XX4

```
0[  ]    0[  ]
1[  ]    1[  ]
2[  ]    2[  ]
3[  ]    3[  ]
4[  ]    4[  ]
5[  ]    5[  ]
6[  ]    6[  ]
7[  ]    7[  ]
8[  ]    8[  ]
9[  ]    9[  ]
```

26.   123   571   113   17X   X23

0[ ]	0[ ]
1[ ]	1[ ]
2[ ]	2[ ]
3[ ]	3[ ]
4[ ]	4[ ]
5[ ]	5[ ]
6[ ]	6[ ]
7[ ]	7[ ]
8[ ]	8[ ]
9[ ]	9[ ]

Answers to practice exercises

Sentence sequence (page 61)

1   1,3,4,2
2   1,3,4,2
3   1,4,3,2
4   3,1,2,4
5   2,1,3,4
6   2,4,1,3
7   2,4,3,1
8   3,2,1,4
9   4,1,3,2
10   3,2,1,4
11   2,4,1,3
12   3,1,4,2
13   3,2,4,1
14   3,2,4,1

Data interpretation (page 67)

1   1
2   3
3   4
4   3
5   1
6   4
7   3

8	2
9	3
10	4
11	1
12	1

Word link (page 72)

1	golf club
2	ship hospital
3	manage regulate
4	top bottom
5	king palace
6	construct retire
7	horse bench
8	agree dispute
9	emperor empire
10	horse hair
11	car petrol
12	light dark
13	anarchy order
14	red green
15	Asia Europe
16	competent defective
17	sketch appraises

Number sequences (page 74)

1	59
2	12
3	44
4	99
5	40
6	92
7	62
8	09
9	08
10	10
11	12
12	08
13	19

14	14
15	11
16	50
17	20
18	40
19	60
20	06
21	10
22	10
23	31
24	81
25	24
26	19

Chapter 5

Mock Test

Over the page you will find a mock test which comprises example questions of the four sub-tests which currently make up the Executive Officer qualifying exam and some parts of the Fast Stream test. Note that the mock test has fewer questions and, consequently, you are allowed less time than in the real exam.

I have deliberately omitted instructions as to how you should approach each of the sub-tests. Before you start you should have studied the RAS guide to the Executive Officer qualifying test and undertaken the practice questions both in the RAS guide and in this book. As a result of this practice, you should be familiar with the demands of each of the sub-tests. If you start and find that you cannot remember what the tests require of you then abandon the exercise and go back over the instructions. This is important because it helps you to cope with any nervousness and allows you to concentrate on the questions.

You are allowed 20 minutes in which to complete the 43 questions. Set a watch or clock so that you can time yourself. Do not turn the page until you are ready to begin. Work as quickly as you can without rushing. Remember that to do well in a test requires you to try hard. You will find the answers at the end of the chapter.

Mock Test

Sentence sequence questions

1.   1.   Befuddled, she made her way to the door, not knowing who it could be at this hour.

  2.   Suddenly, Collette was rudely awakened from her dream by an insistent knocking.

  3.   She had won the national lottery and was about to receive the cheque for two million pounds from the television personality Joanna Lumley.

  4.   Her heart nearly missed a beat when she saw the tall bespectacled man in the leather trenchcoat outside.

1[ ]	1[ ]	1[ ]	1[ ]
2[ ]	2[ ]	2[ ]	2[ ]
3[ ]	3[ ]	3[ ]	3[ ]
4[ ]	4[ ]	4[ ]	4[ ]

2.   1.   This decline is mainly due to a collapse this century in the price of tin

  2.   Tin-mining has been a major industry in Cornwall for over 2,500 years.

  3.   However, there is now only one operating tin mine left in Cornwall.

  4.   In ancient times the Phoenicians traded tin with the Cornish.

1[ ]	1[ ]	1[ ]	1[ ]
2[ ]	2[ ]	2[ ]	2[ ]
3[ ]	3[ ]	3[ ]	3[ ]
4[ ]	4[ ]	4[ ]	4[ ]

3.   1.   After all, the person behind you has been a learner too.

2.   Don't let the fact that you are the first in the queue influence your judgement about when to go on.

3.   What you see when you look must decide your action and nothing else.

4.   As a learner you will be conscious of other drivers lining up behind you at junctions.

1[ ]	1[ ]	1[ ]	1[ ]
2[ ]	2[ ]	2[ ]	2[ ]
3[ ]	3[ ]	3[ ]	3[ ]
4[ ]	4[ ]	4[ ]	4[ ]

4.   1.   This was the media response to the Preliminary Report on Homicide.

2.   The picture painted by the report itself is more complicated.

3.   'The mentally ill commit one murder a fortnight' proclaimed the headlines.

4.   Home Office records suggest that 89 people with probable mental illness committed a murder between 1992 and 1993, more than one a fortnight and 12% of all murders.

1[ ]	1[ ]	1[ ]	1[ ]
2[ ]	2[ ]	2[ ]	2[ ]
3[ ]	3[ ]	3[ ]	3[ ]
4[ ]	4[ ]	4[ ]	4[ ]

5. 1. Input the relevant data, carry out a spell-check and print the document.
    2. Turn on the computer and monitor, key in your pass word and ensure you have entered the word-processing software.
    3. Name and save the file to an appropriate floppy disk and exit the program.
    4. Open a document file.

1[ ]	1[ ]	1[ ]	1[ ]
2[ ]	2[ ]	2[ ]	2[ ]
3[ ]	3[ ]	3[ ]	3[ ]
4[ ]	4[ ]	4[ ]	4[ ]

6. 1. A barrister will then be briefed to present the case in court before a judge.
    2. The solicitor may advise that there is a case and write to the opponent's solicitor.
    3. The potential litigant must first see a solicitor for preliminary advice.
    4. If liability is disputed and cannot otherwise be resolved, pleadings will be issued and a date set for a court hearing.

1[ ]	1[ ]	1[ ]	1[ ]
2[ ]	2[ ]	2[ ]	2[ ]
3[ ]	3[ ]	3[ ]	3[ ]
4[ ]	4[ ]	4[ ]	4[ ]

7. 1. In the re-examination, the witness has the opportunity to rectify any damage done in cross-examination.

   2. First, counsel examines his own witness-in-chief to ascertain facts.

   3. There are three stages to examining a witness in court.

   4. The witness is then made available to the opposition for cross-examination in which the witness's version of events is explored, clarified or demolished.

1[ ]	1[ ]	1[ ]	1[ ]
2[ ]	2[ ]	2[ ]	2[ ]
3[ ]	3[ ]	3[ ]	3[ ]
4[ ]	4[ ]	4[ ]	4[ ]

8. 1. Unlike many of his school friends who went to university, his family circumstances denied him any chance of higher education.

   2. However, he was soon back in Manchester on the staff of the *Evening Chronicle*, before transferring to the rival paper, the *Manchester Evening News*, in a move which was to shape his career.

   3. He therefore started work on the *Blackpool Times* at the age of 17.

   4. Educated at Manchester Grammar School, Lord Ardwick reads *The Guardian* every day of his life.

1[ ]	1[ ]	1[ ]	1[ ]
2[ ]	2[ ]	2[ ]	2[ ]
3[ ]	3[ ]	3[ ]	3[ ]
4[ ]	4[ ]	4[ ]	4[ ]

9.   1.   He was the prime mover behind the EuroTEC controversial refinancing package, and his resignation was not unexpected.

     2.   Peter Heitman quit as Chief Executive as EuroTEC completed the final stage of its difficult restructuring plan.

     3.   It caused the entertainment company's shares to rise 4 pence to 126p.

     4.   The announcement stated that his replacement was Mr Montgomery, the ambitious and widely respected financial head of Paymore Bank, the principal lender to the troubled corporation.

1[ ]	1[ ]	1[ ]	1[ ]
2[ ]	2[ ]	2[ ]	2[ ]
3[ ]	3[ ]	3[ ]	3[ ]
4[ ]	4[ ]	4[ ]	4[ ]

10. 1.   If you do, dial the number of the extension you want and you will automatically be connected.

     2.   Alternatively, you must hang on to be dealt with by an operator.

     3.   On certain telephone switchboards a recorded message will answer your call.

     4.   It will ask you if you know the extension you want and whether or not you have a touch-tone phone.

1[ ]	1[ ]	1[ ]	1[ ]
2[ ]	2[ ]	2[ ]	2[ ]
3[ ]	3[ ]	3[ ]	3[ ]
4[ ]	4[ ]	4[ ]	4[ ]

Data interpretation questions

Table

Country	Population (in millions)	Infant mortality per 1,000 births	Total number of births per 1,000	Agricultural area per person (in acres)
1980				
A	10	45	12	0.25
B	6	82	24	0.125
C	50	11	9	0.1
D	3	30	16	1.3
E	21	60	19	0.9
1990				
A	12	33	11	–
B	6.5	68	24	–
C	49	7	9	–
D	3.1	26	18	–
E	23	45	21	–

Key: – =   information not available

11. Which country experienced the highest rate of infant mortality in 1990?

1) E   2) A   3) B   4) C

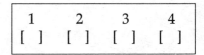

12. Which countries have experienced an increase of two births per 1,000 over the decade?

1) E   D   2) A   C   3) B   C   4) D   A

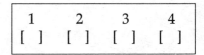

13. What is the percentage increase in population experienced by country E over the decade illustrated?

   1) 10.5%   2) 8.5%   3) 9.0%   4) 9.5%

1	2	3	4
[ ]	[ ]	[ ]	[ ]

14. If in country A the same amount of agricultural land is in use in 1990 as was the case in 1980, to what does the agricultural area per person decrease in 1990 (suggested answers are rounded down to two decimal places)?

   1) 0.20   2) 0.15   3) 0.30   4) none of these

1	2	3	4
[ ]	[ ]	[ ]	[ ]

Word link questions

15. NORTH   SOUTH

   Wales Scotland west   Sussex Kent east

16. CONGESTION   INFERENCE

   blockage superior infection   guess inferior conclusion

17. DYE   TAN

   cloth funeral shoe   coffin leather brown

18. METAL   COIN

   wood paper percussion   brass note news

19. SEASONABLE   RESPECTABLE

   untimely decreasing winter   upright pepper disgraceful

20. CENTIMETRE INCH

metre meter meat foot claw gas

21. WEAK GREEN

month strong moon experienced environmental pliable

22. FUNCTION DIGRESS

work deviant immigrate exodus toil deviate

23. BENEVOLENT MALEVOLENT

ridicule compliment compliant defiant hedonism dilapidated

24. METAPHOR SIMILE

pious mystic undevout irreverent devotee jinx

25. IGNORAMUS ILLUMINATION

obfuscation transfer simple modest scarce encyclopedist

26. DEFICIENT MODERATE

modification perfection gluttonous lapse stigma
temperance

27. MALAPROPISM LINGUISTICS

solipsism behaviourism mathematics psychology
communism engineering

28. AMORPHOUS NEBULOUS

abundance shower torrent profusion
harassment enchantment

Number sequence questions

29. 3   9   27   81   XX3

0[ ]	0[ ]
1[ ]	1[ ]
2[ ]	2[ ]
3[ ]	3[ ]
4[ ]	4[ ]
5[ ]	5[ ]
6[ ]	6[ ]
7[ ]	7[ ]
8[ ]	8[ ]
9[ ]	9[ ]

30. 2   4   8   16   32   XX

0[ ]	0[ ]
1[ ]	1[ ]
2[ ]	2[ ]
3[ ]	3[ ]
4[ ]	4[ ]
5[ ]	5[ ]
6[ ]	6[ ]
7[ ]	7[ ]
8[ ]	8[ ]
9[ ]	9[ ]

31. 3   15   75   375   18XX

0[ ]	0[ ]
1[ ]	1[ ]
2[ ]	2[ ]
3[ ]	3[ ]
4[ ]	4[ ]
5[ ]	5[ ]
6[ ]	6[ ]
7[ ]	7[ ]
8[ ]	8[ ]
9[ ]	9[ ]

32.   322   299   276   2XX   230

0[ ]	0[ ]
1[ ]	1[ ]
2[ ]	2[ ]
3[ ]	3[ ]
4[ ]	4[ ]
5[ ]	5[ ]
6[ ]	6[ ]
7[ ]	7[ ]
8[ ]	8[ ]
9[ ]	9[ ]

33.   2   5   9   14   XX

0[ ]	0[ ]
1[ ]	1[ ]
2[ ]	2[ ]
3[ ]	3[ ]
4[ ]	4[ ]
5[ ]	5[ ]
6[ ]	6[ ]
7[ ]	7[ ]
8[ ]	8[ ]
9[ ]	9[ ]

34.   11   12   22   33   34   XX

0[ ]	0[ ]
1[ ]	1[ ]
2[ ]	2[ ]
3[ ]	3[ ]
4[ ]	4[ ]
5[ ]	5[ ]
6[ ]	6[ ]
7[ ]	7[ ]
8[ ]	8[ ]
9[ ]	9[ ]

35.   1   1   2   6   XX   120

0[ ]	0[ ]
1[ ]	1[ ]
2[ ]	2[ ]
3[ ]	3[ ]
4[ ]	4[ ]
5[ ]	5[ ]
6[ ]	6[ ]
7[ ]	7[ ]
8[ ]	8[ ]
9[ ]	9[ ]

36.   1   8   27   64   1XX

0[ ]	0[ ]
1[ ]	1[ ]
2[ ]	2[ ]
3[ ]	3[ ]
4[ ]	4[ ]
5[ ]	5[ ]
6[ ]	6[ ]
7[ ]	7[ ]
8[ ]	8[ ]
9[ ]	9[ ]

37.   2   6   12   20   30   XX

0[ ]	0[ ]
1[ ]	1[ ]
2[ ]	2[ ]
3[ ]	3[ ]
4[ ]	4[ ]
5[ ]	5[ ]
6[ ]	6[ ]
7[ ]	7[ ]
8[ ]	8[ ]
9[ ]	9[ ]

38.   2   8   26   XX   242

0[ ]	0[ ]
1[ ]	1[ ]
2[ ]	2[ ]
3[ ]	3[ ]
4[ ]	4[ ]
5[ ]	5[ ]
6[ ]	6[ ]
7[ ]	7[ ]
8[ ]	8[ ]
9[ ]	9[ ]

39.   1   2   3   5   7   11   XX

0[ ]	0[ ]
1[ ]	1[ ]
2[ ]	2[ ]
3[ ]	3[ ]
4[ ]	4[ ]
5[ ]	5[ ]
6[ ]	6[ ]
7[ ]	7[ ]
8[ ]	8[ ]
9[ ]	9[ ]

40.   XX   2   6   24   120

0[ ]	0[ ]
1[ ]	1[ ]
2[ ]	2[ ]
3[ ]	3[ ]
4[ ]	4[ ]
5[ ]	5[ ]
6[ ]	6[ ]
7[ ]	7[ ]
8[ ]	8[ ]
9[ ]	9[ ]

41. 0   3   8   XX   24   35

0[ ]	0[ ]
1[ ]	1[ ]
2[ ]	2[ ]
3[ ]	3[ ]
4[ ]	4[ ]
5[ ]	5[ ]
6[ ]	6[ ]
7[ ]	7[ ]
8[ ]	8[ ]
9[ ]	9[ ]

42. 1   2   4   4   XX   8   16   16
25   32   36   64

0[ ]	0[ ]
1[ ]	1[ ]
2[ ]	2[ ]
3[ ]	3[ ]
4[ ]	4[ ]
5[ ]	5[ ]
6[ ]	6[ ]
7[ ]	7[ ]
8[ ]	8[ ]
9[ ]	9[ ]

Answers to mock test (page 90)

1	3,2,1,4
2	2,4,3,1
3	4,2,3,1
4	3,1,2,4
5	2,4,1,3
6	3,2,4,1
7	3,2,4,1
8	4,1,3,2
9	2,1,4,3
10	3,4,1,2
11	3
12	1
13	4

14   1
15   west east
16   blockage conclusion
17   cloth leather
18   paper note
19   untimely disgraceful
20   metre foot
21   strong experienced
22   work deviate
23   compliant defiant
24   mystic devotee
25   obfuscation encyclopedist
26   perfection gluttonous
27   behaviourism psychology
28   abundance profusion
29   24
30   64
31   75
32   53
33   20
34   44
35   24
36   25
37   42
38   80
39   13
40   01
41   15
42   09

Chapter 6

Practice for the Fast Stream

A description of the Fast Stream test

The Fast Stream battery was designed to measure the ability of the top 5 per cent of the population. To realise this ambitious aim RAS has developed a set of very demanding tasks set against tight time constraints. High cut-off scores are applied. I have already reported how RAS expects in the region of 11,000 applicants each year and that only 700 of these will pass through the application stage and battery of tests.

Only those who are very good at the types of question contained in the test are going to pass. The candidate who is likely to succeed will have completed the exercises in Chapters 3, 4 and 5 with little difficulty (two of the Fast Stream battery sub-tests are shared with the Executive Officer Qualifying Exam).

Below is a description of the sub-tests which presently make up the Fast Stream battery. This is followed by practice questions, the answers for which are provided at the end of this chapter. The aim is to help ensure that you understand the test demands fully.

The content of the Fast Stream Qualifying Battery 1994/95 comprised the following:

- Verbal organisation
- Mixed sentences
- Data sufficiency
- Dominoes
- Data interpretation
- Logical reasoning

RAS psychologists are constantly updating the test in an effort to maintain its objectivity. Each sub-test contains experimental questions which carry no score but allow the psychologists to assess their value and, if they constitute an improvement, replace older items. In the same way, whole sub-tests are introduced, improved and in time may come to replace older or less predictive parts of the battery.

If you are due to sit the Fast Stream, you should have received a copy of the RAS publication entitled 'Fast Stream entry qualifying test familiarisation booklet'. It is an important and very useful source of information, which you should read with care. Take particular note of the advice given on the way you record answers and the tactics regarding the value of guessing.

For verbal organisation description and practice questions see sentence sequence in Chapter 4. For practice questions and a description of data interpretation, see the sub-test of that name also in Chapter 4.

I am grateful to staff at RAS for allowing me access to Chapter 2 of the Fast Stream Test Manual.

> If you make it through them all, there will be four separate stages to your application: the application forms, the qualifying exams, two days at an assessment centre with group exercises and interviews, and finally a 35-minute interview.

Practice for the Fast Stream test

Mixed sentences

RAS describes this test as a measure of the ability to interpret high-level written language quickly and to improve on its sense by interchanging words. Each question comprises a sentence in which two words need to be interchanged to make it read sensibly.

Be sure that you realise the limitations imposed. You are only allowed to swap two words so that one replaces the other. This means that from where one word is taken the other must be placed. Do not attempt to alter the sentences in any other way.

In total the test takes 34 minutes but this includes time for reading instructions and practice questions. Once this is excluded you are left with 27 minutes to complete the 45 items which make up the test.

Practice exercises

Underline the the two words which must be interchanged to make the sentence read sensibly.

1.   The Health and Safety at Work Act 1976 is securing at aimed your health, safety and welfare.

2.   Unlike most typewriters, when you come to the end of a press on a word processor you do not have to line the return key as the word processor brings the cursor to the next line automatically.

3.   The equal who gets this job will have a firm commitment to person opportunities.

4.   We are a housing London working in north and west association.

5.   Holidays grade from 22 to 30 working days annually according to range and length of service.

6.   Joyce fell kicking into the chair by the phone, back off her working boots, and went back to sleep.

7.   Nouns are things words and can name people, creatures, naming and feelings.

8.   A subject is a group of sentences which all deal with a single paragraph.

9.   In a vault near Paris is kept a small platinum cylinder which serves as the original reference for kilogram standards; copies are sold and made to laboratories worldwide.

10. National Health Service Hospital private have contracts under which they are allowed to top up their

pay to a limit of 10% with extra earnings from consultants practice.

11. In his conference speech the Prime Minister worried to provide nursery places for every four year old; however, privately, the Education Secretary was pledged because her department had estimated each place would cost in the region of £1,500 per annum.

12. The National Heritage Secretary began his speech by saying that, 'There are at present about 30,000 listed buildings of which slightly under 500,000 are grade 1'.

13. Peter Taylor made a virtue of being impressive and his promotion to Chief Executive within three years of joining the company was widely expected but no less predictable.

14. The twenty-four year old grandfather whose lord won a Victoria Cross in the First World War appealed to his fellow peers 'not to let our heads rule our hearts'.

15. Imperial porphyry is an exceptionally ancient stone with royal associations from the hard world because pharaohs and emperors chose it for the material from which to build their tombs.

Information about a career in the Diplomatic Service is available from: Recruitment Section, Personnel Policy Department, Foreign and Commonwealth Office.

If you are interested in working as a European Fast Stream economist or legal trainee full details and an application form are available from RAS.

Dominoes

People most closely associate these exercises with the Fast Stream exam, and they have been used by the Service since the Second World War.

The domino test was designed to measure general intelligence irrespective of educational attainment. Nowadays RAS prefers to describe it as an indicator of non-verbal, deductive reasoning and flexibility of thought.

The total time taken, once you have read instructions, undertaken some practice questions and completed the test, totals some 48 minutes. Excluding the time taken up with reading and practice questions you are allowed 27 minutes in which to complete 39 items.

You will be relieved to know that the test does not involve your having to be able to play the real game of dominoes but simply to recognise patterns and determine how many dots there should be in each half of the incomplete domino. Note that in some instances the tests require you to work the numbers 0–6 in a loop, ie 0, 1, 2, 3, 4, 5, 6, 0, 1. Each of the following practice questions has only one answer.

I am grateful for the assistance of Jon Stephenson in devising the following examples.

Practice exercises
1.

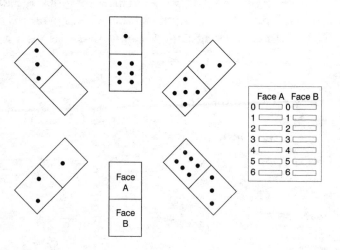

2.

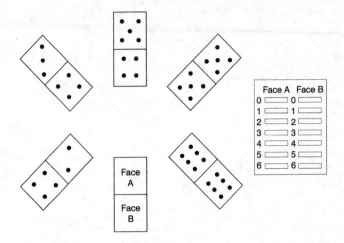

3.

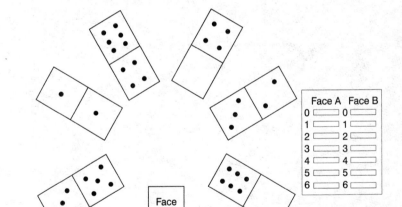

4.

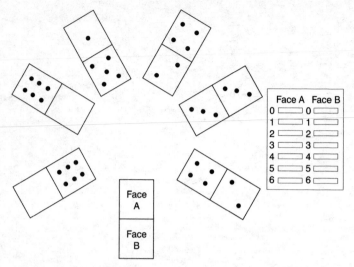

5.

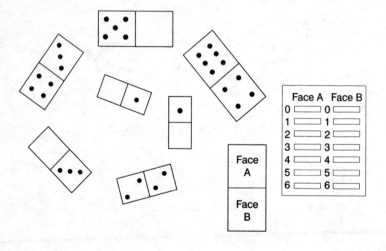

6.

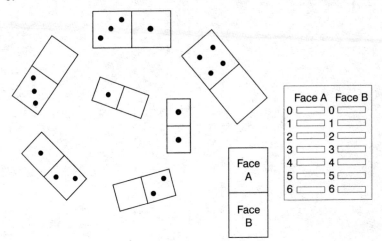

7.

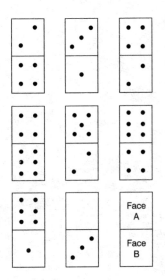

8.

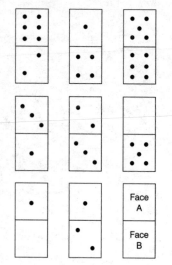

9.

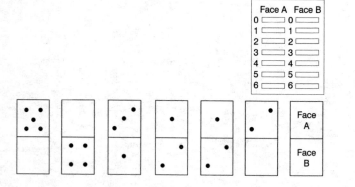

10.

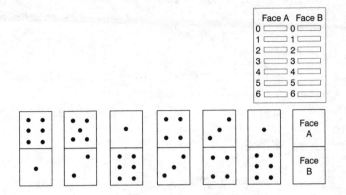

If you want to join the Inland Revenue Fast Stream contact the Inland Revenue Personnel Department.

Data sufficiency

RAS describes this test as a means to measure a candidate's ability to evaluate information and identify logical connections. You are provided with a passage describing a situation and a problem. You are also given a list of 5 additional pieces of information which may or may not resolve the problem. It is your task to identify the items which solve the problem.

The whole test takes some 77½ minutes of which you spend 66 minutes attempting 30 questions.

It is important that you do not waste time working out the answers but only the identity of the items of information required in order to establish the answer.

Practice exercises

1.   A house plant and decorative pot together retail at the inclusive price of £3.75. Which two pieces of information do you require to establish the price of the pot before tax?

   A   The pot costs twice as much as a non-decorative equivalent.

   B   The pot costs three times as much as the plant which is tax exempt.

   C   VAT in the UK is currently 17.5 per cent.

   D   An inclusive total is established by multiplying the exclusive price by the percentage rate of tax and adding this figure to the total.

   E   The price of an item excluding tax can be worked out from the inclusive total by multiplying by 0.036 and subtracting the answer from the total.

   A ⬜   B ⬜   C ⬜   D ⬜   E ⬜

2.   A group of friends charter a yacht for their annual holiday. Which three pieces of information are necessary to establish the amount they each had to contribute towards the deposit?

   A   Because it was the start of the season the trip cost £100; prices increased six-fold by July.

   B   The boat could sleep a maximum of six but one berth will be spare.

   C   The holiday was to last two weeks.

   D   A 10 per cent deposit was payable with the booking and is refundable on the safe return of the vessel.

   E   Tony was going to come but cancelled when he realised the date would clash with his wife's birthday party.

   A ⬜   B ⬜   C ⬜   D ⬜   E ⬜

3. John's 1990 salary was equal to three times his current salary. It was also double what he earned in 1993. Which piece of information do you require in order to establish the percentage decrease he has had to endure since 1990?

    A   Inflation over the period totalled 13 per cent.
    B   John paid £5,250 tax in 1990.
    C   The difference between John's salary in 1990 and 1993 totalled £7,000.
    D   The rate of tax in 1990 was 25 per cent.
    E   John's total current salary was only £1750 greater than his 1990 tax bill.

    A ⬜ B ⬜ C ⬜ D ⬜ E ⬜

4. Peter lives on a small island a short distance off the mainland. His journey to work involves a boat trip and a train journey. Which two pieces of information do you require in order to establish the distance between Peter's house and the railway station?

    A   The channel between the island and mainland is 300 yards across.
    B   It is exactly 400 metres from Peter's house to the pub.
    C   The railway station is on the shore and Peter can see it from his front garden.
    D   The locations of the house, pub and railway station form an equilateral triangle.
    E   The only other building on Peter's island is a pub.

    A ⬜ B ⬜ C ⬜ D ⬜ E ⬜

5.   Donna, Lucy and Chris between them own 80 marbles. Which two pieces of information allow you to establish how many of the marbles are Chris's?

A   Chris and Lucy have the same number.
B   Donna owns twice as many as Lucy.
C   Lucy use to have 25 until she gave some to her brother.
D   Fred, Lucy's brother, has three fewer than twice as many as Donna.

A ⬚ B ⬚ C ⬚ D ⬚ E ⬚

6.   A piece of gold weighing 38 grams is not pure but mixed with base metals. Which three pieces of information do you need to establish the current market value of the gold?

A   80 per cent of the weight is due to the base metal.
B   The base metal is copper.
C   To convert from grams to ounces multiply by 0.03527.
D   The volume of the piece is 3 cubic centimetres.
E   Gold is worth £200 an ounce.

A ⬚ B ⬚ C ⬚ D ⬚ E ⬚

7.   Steven, Kathy and Gino are all to drive from their home town to Springville for an evening out. Gino in his GTi drives at 100 mph, Kathy in her 2CV more sensibly averages 35 mph while Steve never exceeds the speed limit of 60 mph. Which item of information do you require to establish the distance between their home town and Springville?

A   Gino arrived in Springville 5 minutes before Steve and 10 minutes before Kathy.
B   Despite all the stops at traffic lights Kathy completed the journey in 35 minutes.
C   Gino was booked for speeding.
D   Steve completed the journey in 30 minutes.

A ⬚ B ⬚ C ⬚ D ⬚ E ⬚

8. The town hall can accommodate 40 rows of seats with between 25 and 37 seats per row. Which three items of information do you require to establish the percentage of the town's population which can be seated in the town hall when full?

A 20 of the rows can hold over 28 seats.

B The 1991 census of population recorded the town as having a population of 22,350.

C The front 30 rows hold a total of 780 seats (an average of 26 per row).

D Since the closure of the shoe factory and the loss of 1,800 jobs people have moved away leaving the population now 7 per cent below the census total.

E In 1991 18 per cent of the population were under five years of age.

F The overall average number of seats per row is 28.

A ⬜ B ⬜ C ⬜ D ⬜ E ⬜

9. Ford sell their basic 'Model T' at £4,250 or, with extras, for £5,050. Which item of information do you require to establish the most profitable option?

A The price difference between the options totals £800.

B Ford aim at achieving a profit margin of 3 per cent.

C The current basic model comes standard with items sold as extras 18 months ago.

D The basic model achieves the 3 per cent profit margin

E Competition with Japanese car manufactures means that Ford have to supply the extras to customers at cost price.

A ⬜ B ⬜ C ⬜ D ⬜ E ⬜

10. In her will Claire's instructions stated that all her possessions were to be sold and the cash shared out as follows: her second child was to receive £1,000 more than her third child, while her first born was to get three times as much as her second. Which three items of information are required to establish how much Martin was to receive?

A   Sue received £3,500.

B   Claire had four children.

C   Martin is 18 months older than Sue and one year younger than Peter.

D   Ken, Claire's youngest, was born two years after Sue.

E   The children mentioned in the will are called Sue, Peter and Martin.

F   Tragically, Claire outlived one of her children.

A ⬚   B ⬚   C ⬚   D ⬚   E ⬚

For a copy of the booklet 'Fast Stream Administrators and Managers', contact RAS.

Logical reasoning

With this test RAS are keen to establish your ability to handle complex written information and whether you are able to distinguish between what is implied and what is stated.

Each question makes a statement relating to a passage. It is your task to say whether the statement is necessarily true or false or if you cannot tell if it is true or false. You must base your decision only on the information contained in the passage which you are expected to accept as completely true.

The whole test lasts 54½ minutes; excluding time for reading and practice you have 45 minutes in which to attempt 27 questions.

Practice questions

Passage 1
To activate the alarm in the computer department you enter the code 1234. The code 2345 provides cover for the print room as well as the computer department. Code 3456 activates the alarm for the whole building, while 4567 covers the sections for accounts and personnel. Staff are only allowed to know the number for the whole building and the department in which they work. In addition to 3456, Scott and Betty have to remember 4567.

Questions

1. Scott and Betty work in the same department.

True ⬜ False ⬜ Not possible to say ⬜

2. The maximum number of codes staff have to remember is two.

True ⬜ False ⬜ Not possible to say ⬜

3. The code 2345 provides protection for the print room only.

True ⬜ False ⬜ Not possible to say ⬜

Passage 2
Peter shared a father with Hilary but it is not Steven the father of John, youngest son of Silvia (who is Hilary's mother).

Questions

4. Silvia had three children.

True ⬜ False ⬜ Not possible to say ⬜

5. Steven is the father of at least two of Silvia's children.

True ⬜ False ⬜ Not possible to say ⬜

6. Silvia is Peter's mother.

True ⬜ False ⬜ Not possible to say ⬜

7. John was the offspring of Steven and Silvia.

   True [_____] False [_____] Not possible to say [_____]

Passage 3

All scientific statements that are valid state something which is shown by its proof to be so.

Questions

8. The passage demonstrates that all valid statements are scientific.

   True [_____] False [_____] Not possible to say [_____]

9. A valid scientific statement must have a proof.

   True [_____] False [_____] Not possible to say [_____]

10. To be scientific a statement must be valid.

    True [_____] False [_____] Not possible to say [_____]

11. A valid scientific statement must state something.

    True [_____] False [_____] Not possible to say [_____]

Passage 4

The results of subtracting the square of one number from the square of a second gives the same number as is obtained by adding the two numbers, subtracting the first from the second and then multiplying the results of these two calculations.

Questions

12. Whatever the values the same number is obtained.

    True [_____] False [_____] Not possible to say [_____]

13. The first number is the same as the second.

    True [_____] False [_____] Not possible to say [_____]

14. You could divide instead of multiply and get the same answer.

    True ⬚⬚⬚ False ⬚⬚⬚ Not possible to say ⬚⬚⬚

Passage 5

Nothing can arise out of nothing and matter cannot vanish but only be altered to take another form.

Questions

15. If you weigh something, burn it, then weigh it again the difference is the weight of the smoke.

    True ⬚⬚⬚ False ⬚⬚⬚ Not possible to say ⬚⬚⬚

16. There is a finite amount of matter in the universe.

    True ⬚⬚⬚ False ⬚⬚⬚ Not possible to say ⬚⬚⬚

17. It is impossible for the amount of diamonds in the universe to decrease.

    True ⬚⬚⬚ False ⬚⬚⬚ Not possible to say ⬚⬚⬚

18. The amount of matter in the universe will neither increase nor decrease.

    True ⬚⬚⬚ False ⬚⬚⬚ Not possible to say ⬚⬚⬚

19. It should be possible to achieve the alchemists' dream of turning base metals into gold.

    True ⬚⬚⬚ False ⬚⬚⬚ Not possible to say ⬚⬚⬚

For the brochure 'Graduate Careers in the Tax Inspectorate' contact the Inland Revenue Personnel Directorate.

Answers to practice exercises

Mixed sentences (page 105)
1   securing aimed
2   line press
3   equal person
4   London association
5   grade range
6   kicking back
7   things naming
8   subject paragraph
9   sold made
10   private consultants
11   worried pledged
12   30,000 500,000
13   impressive predictable
14   grandfather lord
15   ancient hard

Dominoes (page 108)
1   A:0 B:1
2   A:6 B:1
3   A:2 B:5
4   A:1 B:5
5   A:0 B:0
6   A:4 B:1
7   A:1 B:6
8   A:2 B:4
9   A:6 B:3
10   A:2 B:5

Data sufficiency (page 113)
1   B,C
2   A,B,D
3   C
4   B,D
5   A,B
6   A,C,E
7   B
8   B,D,F

9   E
10   A,C,E

Logical reasoning (page 118)
1   Not possible to say
2   False
3   False
4   Not possible to say
5   Not possible to say
6   Not possible to say
7   True
8   False
9   True
10   False
11   True
12   True
13   Not possible to say
14   False
15   Not possible to say
16   Not possible to say
17   False
18   True
19   Not possible to say

If you suffer a disability which might affect your test performance telephone RAS and discuss it with them prior to the test day.

Further Information

RAS can be contacted at:

Alencon Link
Basingstoke
Hampshire RG21 1JB

Tel: 01256 846354

or

24 Whitehall
London SW1A 2ED

Tel: 0171 210 6689

Further Reading from Kogan Page

Great Answers to Tough Interview Questions, 3rd edition, Martin John Yate, 1992
How to Pass Computer Selection Tests, Sanjay Modha, 1994
How to Pass Graduate Recruitment Tests, Mike Bryon, 1994
How to Pass Selection Tests, Mike Bryon and Sanjay Modha, 1991
How to Pass Technical Selection Tests, Mike Bryon and Sanjay Modha, 1993
Interviews Made Easy, Mark Parkinson, 1994
Test Your Own Aptitude, 2nd edition, Jim Barrett and Geoff Williams, 1990

In preparation:
How to Pass Numeracy Tests
How to Pass Verbal Reasoning Tests